Unconventional Crises, Unconventional Responses: Reforming Leadership in the Age of Catastrophic Crises and Hypercomplexity

By

Erwan Lagadec

Lagadec, Erwan, *Unconventional Crises, Unconventional Responses: Reforming Leadership in the Age of Catastrophic Crises and Hypercomplexity* (Washington, D.C.: Center for Transatlantic Relations, 2007).

Center for Transatlantic Relations
The Paul H. Nitze School of Advanced International Studies
The Johns Hopkins University
1717 Massachusetts Ave., NW, Suite 525
Washington, D.C. 20036
Tel. (202) 663-5880
Fax (202) 663-5879
Email: transatlantic@jhu.edu
http://transatlantic.sais-jhu.edu

ISBN 10: 0-9788821-8-0
ISBN 13: 978-0-9788821-8-1

Cover picture: Albrecht Dürer (1471-1528), "The Four Horsemen of the Apocalypse" (detail), Rosenwald Collection, image courtesy of the Board of Trustees, National Gallery of Arts, Washington, D.C.

Table of Contents

This is a new kind of war!
We are not ready for *this*!

—*A NORAD official, September 11, 2001*

Acknowledgments

This project is based on the premise that we must dare to think, prepare, and act against the grain of conventional wisdom in the face of catastrophic crises. Over the past year I have been fortunate enough to count on the support and leadership of individuals and organizations who not only agreed with this proposition, but were eager to act upon it, even at a time when doing so amounted to a leap in the dark.

My warmest thanks go to Dr. Esther Brimmer and Dr. Daniel Hamilton, who welcomed me at the Center for Transatlantic Relations (CTR) in the summer of 2006.

Pierre Béroux, Directeur du Contrôle des Risques at Electricité de France, showed unshakable faith in the value of the project; his financial support was critical in overcoming obstacles that a pilot-project such as this inevitably encounters. At Verizon, J. Michael Hickey also ensured the financial viability of the project, and remained an attentive observer and insightful adviser throughout the course of its development. We also wish to thank Accor North America, Société Générale, and the American Red Cross for their generous contributions.

The organization of our unconventional seminar in March 2007 was an administrative and logistical tour-de-force, which was only made possible thanks to the competence and patience of CTR's Gretchen Losee and Katrien Maes. The reception hosted by Mr. Kevin O'Shea, Minister for Political Affairs at the Canadian Embassy in Washington, D.C., was a highlight of our event, and provided an occasion to acknowledge the crucial contribution of Canadian partners in the project: our thanks to Katie Tolan and her colleagues for putting it together.

The unconventional format and short timeframe of our project brought unusual demands on our participants. The success of the project, first and foremost, is theirs. Our thanks go most especially to those who traveled from Europe to attend the seminar, and to session coordinators who agreed to share with us the burden of ensuring that our roundtable discussions remained outside-the-box, while safeguarding their coherence. Through their unparalleled expertise, their taste for open intellectual enquiry, as well as their encouragements and friendship, Nan Buzard, Mike Granatt, and James Young made an especially valuable contribution to our efforts.

In what follows, I have strived to remain faithful to the thrust of our participants' arguments, and convey a sense of the striking commonalities in their outlooks, without obscuring their occasional differences. While I hope to have provided a fair reflection of their views, I am of course solely responsible for the contents of the report.

Erwan Lagadec
Washington, D.C.
December 2007

Introduction

The Need for Inter-Sector and International Dialogue

Since the 1990s, North America and Europe have confronted a series of unconventional, catastrophic, or "hypercomplex" crises. On the one hand, the U.S. and Canada have faced the 1998 ice storm, 9/11, the anthrax crisis, the SARS outbreak in Toronto, the 2003 Northeast blackout, and Hurricane Katrina. In the meantime, Europe has been hit by the "Mad Cow" disease, 1999 storms in France, 2002 floods in Central Europe, 2003 heatwave in France and Italy, and 2007 forest fires in Greece; in addition, both sides of the Atlantic responded to the 2004 Indian Ocean tsunami.

These events have shared striking similarities, especially inasmuch as they destabilized leaders in charge of response and reconstruction efforts. Clearly, therefore, the time has come to launch a high-level, balanced dialogue among North American and European leaders, analysts and experts, representing the public, private, and humanitarian sectors, with the goal of enabling a detailed and long-term exchange among their respective experiences, unresolved questions, intuitions, and proposals for reform.

Reforming Traditional "Crisis Management"

Recent catastrophic crises repeatedly have overwhelmed traditional mechanisms for crisis planning and management, and have made them instantly obsolete, in several respects.

The challenge of the "unthinkable." This series of events has clearly shown that complex Western societies today are not equipped to confront major crises effectively. The basic concepts and tools defined from the 1980s onward in the field of crisis management fall short of what is needed today. Current mechanisms for anticipation and response were designed to confront an event circumscribed to a specific area, within a global system that otherwise remained stable: but we lack a radar screen and a method to deal with crises that destabilize entire systems. This is *the* crucial challenge of our times. "Category 5" events today occur with unprecedented frequency—literally with respect to meteorology, but metaphorically in every other critical field as well. Moreover, because of structural characteristics of modern societies, e.g. strategic interdependencies, global connections, constant acceleration of causal chains, and the risk of "liquefaction" of our systems' foundations (i.e. the unthinkable collapse of trusted systems hit by unconventional events), massive destabilization can be provoked not only by catastrophic events, but also by crises that initially seem mundane, and would have remained so in the recent past.

The culture of leaders. Generally speaking, in all countries and sectors, they have proved culturally incapable of taking the "unthinkable" seriously, let alone react effectively when it actually occurred. They tend to eschew the challenges posed by unconventional events, in large part because those fall outside the intellectual principles that frame organizational architectures and "normal" decision-making, and that underlie the selection of leaders in the first place. In this context, the very mention of unconventional risks and crises tends to provoke considerable uneasiness and reluctance. Cultural, analytical and even psychological obstacles thus compound the challenge at stake.

The identity of leaders. The public sector's traditional monopoly on planning and response efforts time and again has shown its limits when confronted with unconventional events. The priority now must be to define new allocations of tasks and responsibilities among the public, private, and humanitarian sectors, as well as the wider public : a new "Social Contract," without which the democratic foundations of Western societies themselves are at risk, as Hurricane Katrina has shown.

Complex maps of actors. Catastrophic crises systematically involve an enormous variety of stakeholders, on an international scale (as for instance during the 2004 Tsunami). These include spontaneous, unanticipated coalitions among unlikely partners on one end of the spectrum, as well as individuals that can wield extraordinary and unexpected power, especially through the channels of "old" and "new" media alike, at the other end. This complexity makes it near impossible for "traditional" leaders to plan, let alone coordinate response efforts.

New processes for crisis recovery. Today's unconventional crises generally do not contrast a single "Ground Zero" with an unscathed "outside" from which response can be safely organized: on the contrary, they destabilize systems in their entirety. Therefore, instead of a clear succession of phases from planning to response to reconstruction (each under the leadership of a different agent, which withdraws and transitions to the next when its job is done), leaders now must tackle the three together, and ideally build reconstruction dynamics into their contingency plans (as Iraq demonstrates *a contrario*)—all the while taking into account that *leaders and responders themselves* might be among the victims of unconventional crises.

The Project

Unorthodox characteristics. Confronting unconventional crises requires not only unconventional modes of preparation, planning and response, but also (in the first place) unconventional and innovative analytical methods.

Most often, specialists and leaders are content with sharing and validating case-specific "best practices," rather than developing a global analysis of the emerging challenges posed by catastrophic crises *of all kinds*. Furthermore, in spite of constant (and fashionable) calls for "returns of experience," "benchmarking," or the "sharing of best practices," exceedingly few projects actually go beyond run-of-the-mill cataloguing of facts and professorial descriptions of "proven" ("sellable?") methods.

In the same way, beyond fashionable slogans, genuine efforts to build bridges (other than one-way) among different outlooks remain few and far between. Most specialized events do not in fact enable a balanced dialogue among academics, experts, and operational leaders; among the public, private, and humanitarian sectors; and between continents. Symposia and conferences all too often merely juxtapose professorial interventions from "authoritative" experts whose viewpoints bounce off each other, rather than intermingle and cross-fertilize. This is certainly not conducive to shared innovation.

A network of networks. In the summer 2006, an opportunity emerged to act on these several "diagnoses," and organize a transatlantic network that would genuinely open up a space for balanced dialogue among North American and European specialists: that would (at least in a first phase) put more onus on unresolved questions than on pre-formatted answers, more emphasis on innovation (even audacity) than on rigid methodological, bibliographical, or semantic concerns; lead to the creation of a joint platform for reflection and action, in which partners from different backgrounds and countries would work together rather than talk past each other; and take transatlantic factors seriously, i.e. highlight mutual vulnerabilities, common challenges, and potential strengths.

Based on a common assessment of the challenges at hand, and the complementarity of their respective networks, the Center for Transatlantic Relations at the Paul H. Nitze School of Advanced International Studies (Johns Hopkins University) in Washington, D.C., launched a partnership with Patrick Lagadec (Ecole Polytechnique) in Paris, with financial support from Electricité de France's Direction du Contrôle des Risques, and Verizon's bureau for Public Policy Development and National Security.

The project titled "Unconventional Crises, Unconventional Responses: Reforming Leadership in the Age of Catastrophic Crises and 'Hypercomplexity'" was born from this rapprochement in the summer of 2006.

Both parties combined and built upon their respective high-level networks among public, private and humanitarian sector leaders, as well as academic experts, in North America and Europe: from e.g. the United Nations, the Department of Homeland Security, the UK's Cabinet Office, the American Red Cross, and major critical infrastructure providers, to Homeland Security specialists from influential think-tanks such as the Center for Strategic and International Studies in the U.S., or the International Institute for Strategic Studies in Britain.

A Survey of Unconventional Crises

Each of our participants brought to the project firsthand experience of crises that they thought had most critically overwhelmed traditional response mechanisms. Their recollections and analyses produced an impressive overview of recent catastrophic and hypercomplex events, in several respects: first, it involved crises that had occurred world-wide; second, these events were extremely varied in character, but tended to challenge response systems and leaders in similar, or at least mutually recognizable ways; third, they ranged from major events so clearly catastrophic in nature that they have become the "icons" of and shorthand for what such events "look like," to insidious destabilizations and initially mundane occurrences that triggered unexpected, complex snowball effects.

Catastrophic Events

In recent history, there is no doubt that the "three horsemen of the Apocalypse" that best illustrate the impact and consequences of catastrophic events, for leaders, analysts, and popular culture alike, are September 11, the 2004 Indian Ocean Tsunami, and Hurricane Katrina. These three events elicited by far the most mentions from our participants.

Some were affected directly by the sheer scale of 9/11. A private sector leader, whose firm is based in lower Manhattan, had to account for no fewer than 400 employees, including some that he knew had been in the World Trade Center itself or in the area nearby at the time of the attacks. Indeed, he recalled that other companies were confronted with an even more daunting challenge, having to locate several thousands of their employees. As other participants pointed out, the scale of 9/11 was such that it provoked unlikely ground shifts at a systemic level, such as the reshuffling of the entire Homeland Security administration in the U.S., and the reform of rules of operation in the airline and airport business internationally.

However, in terms of geography and critical infrastructure capabilities, even 9/11 is dwarfed by Katrina. Although some participants went through the storm relatively unscathed, as they had positioned their assets on higher ground, not all could do so. Wireline and wireless companies struggled to restore systems that were essentially annihilated. Humanitarian organizations accustomed to dealing with disasters on an international scale did not manage to meet the public's expectation, or their own, in this case. Bluntly put by a participant, the challenges raised by Katrina were so overwhelming that all responders met a "fair share of successes and extreme failures": all the more so as Katrina was not in fact an isolated event, but was followed almost immediately by Hurricanes Rita in Texas and Wilma in Florida—which only compounded the challenge for participants that had assets in all three areas.

The 2004 Tsunami was of course the ultimate behemoth, causing 230,000 deaths from Indonesia to Somalia. In the U.S. and European private sectors, the tourism industry was of course hardest hit, losing guests, employees, as well as scores of hotels. The response of Western countries, though initially characterized as "stingy," was ultimately staggering. A participant recalled that the U.S. Congress eventually appropriated about $647 million to assist in response efforts, while the private sector in the U.S. raised no less than $2 billion—a sum which had to be capped as private companies were not properly positioned to manage its effective and controlled disbursement across the affected areas.

Going back in time, the 1962 North Sea Flood destroyed the homes of about 60,000 people in Northern Germany, as far as 60 miles (100 km) inland. In 1986, the scale of the Chernobyl accident was such that it could not be hidden or spun even by the Soviet propaganda machine, in spite of its best efforts, vis-à-vis both foreign and domestic publics. Chernobyl therefore provides a peculiar, but in part universally valid example of the way in which unconventional events do much more than affect a "Ground Zero," but also destabilize entire systems, including through the loss of trust and the "liquefaction" of social contracts among leaders and the greater public.

Insidious Events

At the opposite end of the spectrum from such highly visible, iconic crises of catastrophic proportions, some events are equally unconventional because they remain insidious, under radar screens and alarm thresholds, and are prone to be mislabeled or underestimated.

The flu pandemic in many respects belongs to this category: spikes of concern and intense research regularly give way to ill-advised nonchalance, caused both by the mistaken belief that periods of heightened concern have led to the finalization of all necessary plans, and by a "cry wolf" lassitude that leads some among the greater public and even leaders to dismiss the pandemic risk altogether. While the risk posed by the event itself is not properly flagged, the same would apply to its consequences: the pandemic would not produce instant catastrophic effects, but slow and indirect decays in our systems. The nightmare of planners and decision-makers is the capacity of individual wills and passions to compromise their own capacity to anticipate the circumstances and effects of proposed actions: yet in the case of the flu pandemic, *everything* will be a matter of individual human fears, impressions, and trust. How does one plan, as a participant put it, for a "general malaise," in a context where leaders in government, the private sector and humanitarian organizations cannot trust the coherence of each other's response over time and across countries (given the poor visibility available), and therefore cannot make coherent decisions themselves? How does one prepare for an event when it is unclear whether it "is happening" or not, or who can make this judgment?

For too long, of course, even HIV-AIDS remained below alert thresholds. In many countries it is still a catastrophic event that does not say its name. As a participant pointed out, in Southern Africa up to one in three people are infected with AIDS; the average life expectancy has fallen from the mid-60s to little more than 40 years. The direct and indirect impact of this crisis on economies, as well as social, community, and business structures, will of course be profound —yet will remain murky, confusing, and poorly understood. In many parts of the world, malnutrition is an even more critical example of a crisis that only elicits distracted attention, all the while unraveling the fabric of societal systems, and therefore paving the way for more aggressive and visible catastrophic events.

At first sight, the foot-and-mouth crisis that hit the UK in 2001 does not fall into the same category, as it was clearly flagged as a considerable threat, and indeed has yielded iconic images of extreme (some might say, excessive) reactions from government leaders. Yet, in this particular case, the problem is that authorities identified the "wrong" crisis, while the "real" catastrophic event thrived out of sight and under the radar. As one of our participants explained, the British government failed to realize that while it was busy defending the live-stock industry, i.e. 0.5 percent of GDP and 12 percent of the rural economy, by turning vast swaths of the countryside into "no-go" areas, it was destroying tourism, which amounts to 5 percent of the UK's GDP, and 80 percent of its rural economy. "It took the government three weeks to realize that—three long weeks."

Cascading Events

As was noted earlier in this report, the characteristics of today's globalized world are such that events which by themselves would seem mundane (at least in comparison with unmistakably catastrophic crises such as 9/11, Katrina or the 2004 Tsunami), and indeed would have remained so in the recent past, can now trigger unforeseen snowball effects and lead to considerable systemic destabilizations.

Physical interdependencies among critical infrastructure systems are the most obvious examples of this phenomenon—though by no means the most threatening. For instance, the Northeast blackout of 2003 originated with a single plant near Cleveland, Ohio; yet the cas-cading effect that resulted ultimately forced the shutdown of more than 100 power plants, causing an outage that affected no fewer than 60 million people in Canada and the U.S., and financial costs esti-mated at $6 billion. A potentially similar cascading effect was recently averted when an undersea cable critically important to international telecommunications was successfully repaired, after it had been destroyed in an earthquake in East Asia.

However, more complex (and ultimately, dangerous) interdependen-cies connect not only physical equipments, but multiple sectors of the economy, building blocks of our polities, and even public perceptions: in other words, the foundations upon which our entire systems are built.

As one of our participants recalled, a major U.S. food company suffered considerable losses at the end of the 1990s through the failure of its leadership to recognize an emerging issue while it was still man-ageable, i.e. before it turned into a fully fledged crisis. A few consumers in Europe became sick after consuming its product; the company reacted by dismissing the importance of the incident. However, circumstances in the affected country happened to create a perfect environment to magnify a fairly trivial event into a crisis that ended up having a significant impact on the company. Unfortunately, awareness of that fact never reached headquarters in the U.S., which persisted in dismissing the incident as a local issue. By the time the U.S. hierarchy finally came to realize that the problem had mushroomed beyond control, the company was on the verge of losing several hundred million dollars worth of market shares worldwide.

Even more critically, in 2000, a handful of protesters nearly brought the British economy to its knees in a matter of days, against all expectations, by blockading fuel supplies in some areas of the country. Ripple-effects occurred through the most convoluted and unforeseen channels. As a participant explained, "even though they had priority for fuel, hospital wards were shutting: the reason was that schools were shutting, because teachers didn't have fuel. If schools shut, children don't go to school; if children don't go to school, working mothers stay at home; and a great number of the senior nursing staff in the UK's public health service are working mothers." Here again, the speed of cascading effects brought about by network interdependencies was considerably underestimated by leaders in charge, in this case the British government.

Such instantaneous, complex, and confusing "domino effects" demonstrate that response efforts to catastrophic or hypercomplex crises do not deal with a single affected framework ("ground zero"), or even with an interconnected chain of destabilized frameworks: but with "sickened" dynamics and movements *within them*. Metaphorically, as a participant put it, the networks that affect us today comprise not only the "plumbing," but also the "water that flows through the pipe," i.e. also movement and interactions among people, in ways that can hardly be predicted.

Telecommunications contribute crucially to this "granularity" of crises and their propagation. The public's expectation of being able to communicate with loved ones instantaneously and at all times creates a powerful mechanism for the acceleration and the spread of crisis, confusion and destabilization when an initial event (or the resulting spike in cellphone traffic) compromises wireless communications—as occurred after the London bombings on July 7, 2005, and indeed in the aftermath of most other catastrophic crises.

Loss of trust is another critical trigger of unforeseen cascading effects. Participants mentioned two cases in point. Immediately following the Torrey Canyon oil spill off the coast of England in 1967, authorities across the Channel were quick to claim that the problem did not concern France. Two weeks later, the oil had reached French waters. Affected populations were understandably incensed by the nonchalance of their leaders. From the very first, response efforts had to be organized in the context of a complete loss of trust vis-à-vis government.

Wary of such precedents, a participant from a major utility recalled his concern when, following an incident at a chemical factory which caused thirty fatalities, it transpired that his company could be at fault, as the explosion might have been triggered by a spark in its power supply lines. This hypothesis was only ruled out after more than two years, during which the company struggled to devise an acceptable position on the matter.

Hypercomplex Events

Metaphorically, leaders confronted with unconventional crises find themselves in a position akin to 15th- and 16th-century navigators who sailed beyond "the edge of the world," to areas that their charts did not cover. The main characteristic of unconventional events is that they are exceedingly difficult to map. This can be due to:

- the technical complexity of response efforts

- an unusually complex geography of affected areas

- the potential for a crisis suddenly to affect systems and interests that initially seemed remote (just as a virus jumps "species barriers")

- a bewildering kaleidoscope of stakeholders

- confusing, overwhelming, or, conversely, insufficient information.

Hypercomplexity in unconventional events is not always properly acknowledged. A participant pointed out that following Katrina, many commentators in Europe failed to understand the scale of the challenges posed by the storm, which hit an area the size of Great Britain. They claimed that centralized polities such as France would have responded in a more coherent fashion to such a disaster, by preventing the confusion brought about by the layered political system in the United States, which combines local, state and federal centers of decision. In fact, the prospect of a Katrina-like event in Europe is sobering. Smugness is ill-advised when one considers for instance a situation in which London, Northern France (including nuclear power plants) and the Netherlands simultaneously would find themselves under water, and their leaders had to call for help at once from NATO and the European Union. Clearly the most centralized plans and policies in the world would be instantly overwhelmed, and the resulting confusion would bear much resemblance to Katrina's aftermath.

Technical complexity is the most readily identifiable among these factors. It is particularly acute in the wake of catastrophic crises, as they tend to impact all critical and "human" infrastructures needed in the response effort. September 11, and even more so the 2004 Tsunami and Katrina, presented nearly intractable challenges in this respect, as they undermined communications, transportation systems, and water, food, power, and fuel supplies. They also compromised the normal "architecture" of human resources, as some among the first responders turned out to be victims themselves, while others who were not on duty, as well as non-professional volunteers, decided to take part in response efforts anyway, with little or no control from organizations supposedly "in charge." Following the crash of an airliner in a Middle Eastern country, one of our participants recalled that the local embassy of the European country most severely affected had to cope with families' victims, local authorities, high-level delegations from its capital, and scores of journalists, "with an 'army' of twelve staff." Of course, these challenges would be even more critical in case of a nuclear, radiological, biological, or chemical terrorist attack.

The terrain itself can cause or compound technical complexity. This was the case for instance in the wake of the catastrophic earthquake that hit a remote and mountainous area of Pakistan in the fall of 2005. A participant recalled that the evacuation of French citizens from La Paz, Bolivia in 2004 was put in jeopardy by a lack of transport aircrafts that could safely land at an altitude of almost 12,000 feet. In France itself, following the destructive storms of December 1999, utilities struggled for weeks to restore power to remote villages in areas where entire forests had been downed together with electrical pylons.

Response efforts can also be hampered by politically unstable environments, or even war. Most notably, international intervention following the 2004 Tsunami often had to take in its stride complex and volatile political circumstances, in Aceh as well as Sri Lanka. Participants recalled the difficulties encountered by response or reconstruction efforts in worn-torn Baghdad, and in Lebanon during the 2006 conflict between Hezbollah and Israel.

Finally, the lack of technical knowledge among responders can impede recovery efforts. The 1999 outbreak of the West Nile Virus in the U.S. required spraying the New York City area against mosquitoes: however, local governments had not done so since the days of yellow fever, and therefore had long lost all relevant expertise; nor did they have any of the appropriate equipment.

Purely technical difficulties, however, are only one cause of hypercomplexity in unconventional events: indeed, though easiest to identify and diagnose, they are by no means the most critical. **Complex geography**, for instance, can have much more destabilizing effects on response efforts.

Katrina demonstrates that unconventional crises will not have a single "ground zero." They are not localized wounds that can be closed from the outside in: but rather akin to a global septic shock. Like Katrina, some events are unconventional because they affect several locations simultaneously. In fact, Katrina itself was compounded by the succession of hurricanes Rita and Wilma, which made landfall respectively in Texas and Florida. September 11 was similarly challenging for companies that had assets in New York as well as Virginia, and had to set their response efforts in motion in two, or even three different sites. In September 2005, foreshadowing the situation in Southern Europe two summers later, wildfires erupted in more than a dozen different locations in Southern California, straining the resources of local and out-of-state firefighters to near breaking-point.

In some cases, the challenge arises not from the fact that an actual crisis impacts several sites at once, but because the exact location where a highly probable event will strike in the future is unknown. For instance, private sector companies with significant assets in Florida must protect all of them against hurricanes that are bound to occur, but could make landfall anywhere.

Other crises present hypercomplex geographies because they impact huge areas at once: in addition to Katrina, the 2004 Tsunami has of course become the iconic example of such disturbances, as it affected several thousand miles of coastline in South-East and South Asia, as well as Africa. This posed an unprecedented challenge, including for tourism companies with assets spread across all parts of the impacted area.

Most challenging, however, is the hypercomplexity of crises that undermine all notions of geography, of core and center, because they are near-ubiquitous, or affect movement within networks rather than localized networks themselves. This is especially the case of epidemics such the avian flu—which so far has spread to no fewer than 55 countries. During the 2003 SARS outbreak in Canada, "everybody who got within a hundred miles of Toronto and got a fever later thought they had the disease: Canadian public health authorities spent weeks of manpower time tracking potential cases from virtually every country in the world." The 2001 anthrax crisis, where a quintessentially volatile substance was spread through the quintessential network that is the postal service, has become the ultimate symbol of a crisis that affects flows as well as places, and disrupts an entire system through ubiquitous human anxieties rather than physical destruction. Turning from physical to virtual contagion, the "non-event" of Y2K was of course equally ubiquitous. As a participant emphasized, the Internet presents challenges similar in many respects to epidemics: crises that affect it can be insidious and hard to pinpoint, and blur all clear frameworks as to time, space, and causal chains. In case of a worldwide Internet destabilization, "where do you begin your crisis coordination? Where do you begin your disaster response?"

Y2K and Internet disruptions provide striking examples of crises that can jump systemic barriers and metastasize to other networks and interests, as they threaten to compromise the network that underpins most others in modern societies.

The risks posed by this type of **"cross-systemic" complexity** are most evident when an initial event comes to involve national or international security issues, or threatens to do so. Participants from the Department of Defense or the United Nations witnessed firsthand the immediate conversion of September 11 from a homeland security to a military and international security issue, as policymakers' attention worldwide turned to a potential military response in Afghanistan, and U.S. allies in NATO and elsewhere, as well as the UN Security Council, were brought into play. Another participant highlighted a similar point, when he mentioned his experience on a medical team that was tasked with conducting a forensic inquiry into the suspicious death of a newly-elected African leader, which was threatening to provoke a civil war. In this case, "unthinkably," the stability of a major country, and the strategic balance in the region, came to depend on a medical diagnosis. Again, following a nuclear incident abroad, a participant took a leading role in secret talks between the U.S. government and leaders of the affected country, fully aware that public disclosure of these discussions would critically destabilize the local government, and adversely affect U.S. interests and diplomacy in the region. Again, the enquiry into the Lockerbie disaster soon became entangled with international security and diplomatic considerations.

In the same way that crises can overwhelm firewalls and jump barriers to affect domestic or international politics, they can also mutate into massive economic disruptions. Just as the foot-and-mouth crisis in the UK affected both the agriculture and tourism sectors, the 2003 SARS outbreak in Toronto soon turned from a public health into an economic crisis, especially after the World Health Organization issued an official warning against travel to the city.

Even more fundamentally, an initial event can also transcend its initial context to fray the fabric of social cohesion itself, even in areas which it did not directly affect. For instance, following the attacks on 9/11 in New York, a major challenge for law enforcement officials in the neighboring areas was sometimes to maintain civic order. As one participant recalled, people were being attacked because they "looked Arabic," and mosques were vandalized. Authorities had to broadcast warnings against hate crimes, and toured Muslim communities with the FBI in order to reassure them.

The collapse of "network barriers" is only one among many causes of a common characteristic of all unconventional events, namely the **hypercomplexity of maps of actors**.

Quantitatively, the sheer number of victims and responders is the most conspicuous aspect of this complexity. This of course was the case in the wake of catastrophic events such as 9/11, the 2004 Tsunami,

Katrina, or the massive earthquake that hit Pakistan in October 2005. Similarly, in the summer of 2006, international organizations in Lebanon had to cope with the displacement of up to a million people —as they left their homes to escape the fighting, and then returned after a cease-fire was agreed. Again, in 1999, Kosovo experienced movements of populations on a scale that international officials had not foreseen, especially at the infamous Blace border crossing, where desperate crowds of up to 70,000 evacuees congregated as neighboring Macedonia refused to let them in. In late 2002, the French government had to organize the evacuation of no fewer than 15,000 of its nationals desperate to leave the Ivory Coast, as the country veered towards civil war. In August 2006, Canada was confronted with an equally challenging situation, when it had to evacuate 17,000 of its citizens from war-torn Lebanon.

Aside from the sheer numbers of victims or stakeholders, their *variety* can cause even more acute challenges. Recent experiences in the Balkans, Afghanistan, and Iraq have highlighted the complexity of civil-military relations, and set in motion "transformational" efforts at the U.S. Department of Defense, NATO, and the European Union: yet, they only make up one among many facets of the problem.

The 2004 Tsunami has become the classic example of hypercomplex maps of actors, as it involved a confusing array of public, private, humanitarian, and faith-based responders from every corner of the world, not all of which had the mechanisms or expertise in place to ensure their own effectiveness, or indeed the coherence of the global effort. In the face of this kaleidoscope, governments worldwide proved unable to retain their traditional monopoly on response leadership and coordination: even more so as their credibility was critically undermined by the fact that their investment, in financial and human terms, was dwarfed by that of NGOs and the greater public. The growth of tourism as a global industry is bound to cause the recurrence of similar circumstances in the future, and put at the forefront strategic, cultural, and capability gaps among and between international actors—most notably, Western "countries of origins," and Southern, developing "destination countries."

In the same way, response efforts after Hurricane Katrina were hampered by the lack of coordination among a huge and unforeseen variety of actors, including international organizations and more than sixty foreign countries. As a participant noted, "the U.S. had never expected to be the *recipient* of material aid, and had absolutely no policy or procedures in place for receiving, accounting for, or distributing international donations." Pre-existing partnerships, such as mutual aid agreements among private infrastructure providers or even governments, helped funnel some of the outpouring of solidarity into coherent channels, but most such arrangements had not been designed to tackle a crisis on this scale and were instantly overwhelmed. Even the intricate economic, military, and homeland security ties between the U.S. and Canada had to be supplemented by ad-hoc initiatives from both sides.

Both on 9/11 and "7/7" (the terrorist bombings in London on July 7, 2005), response efforts involved a vast number of stakeholders, including from the private sector, the media and the greater public, which made it near impossible for public sector leaders to set up coordination systems called for by their plans. Indeed Mayor Giuliani's most notable achievement on September 11 is arguably that he managed to rebuild a command-and-control mechanism from the bottom up, using the building blocks that were the multiple sub-networks that tied together private entrepreneurs and citizens, rather than attempting to force a traditional, top-down response "architecture" upon them. Within the U.S. government in Washington, the complexity of stakeholders on that day was equally bewildering. Most U.S. agencies were involved in some capacity in the immediate aftermath of the attacks, and yet had to act quickly, and effectively.

Similarly, in August 2006, all layers of the Canadian government and society at large were challenged by the evacuation of Canadian nationals from Lebanon. The crisis quickly turned from foreign to domestic, as the first evacuees began to arrive back in the country. Triaging and sheltering the returning expatriates came to involve local municipalities, state governments, the private sector (most notably transportation companies and hotel chains), NGOs, and the greater public, in addition to the central government in Ottawa.

Complex maps of actors jeopardize the effectiveness of response efforts in part because actors often come in with different, indeed sometimes mutually exclusive goals and priorities. This was most clearly brought to light during the Southern California wildfires of September-October 2005. Conflicting views soon emerged among the many stakeholders involved (including the private sector, NGOs, and the greater public) as to which geographic areas should get priority; whether the effort should focus on saving homes, or on containing the fire as fast as possible; or whether non-emergency responders who didn't have expertise in responding to wildfires should be utilized in spite of the risks involved. The conflict was most acute between the political and the professional emergency management leadership, at the national, state, and local levels.

Finally, *numbers* and *variety* are not the only factors that account for the complexity of maps of actors in unconventional situations. Their effects are compounded by the unpredictable influence that *individuals* among these actors can exert on the course of events: not only individual leaders or responders, which goes without saying, but individual victims, bystanders, or observers. As we shall see below, in the course of the fuel protests that paralyzed the UK economy in 2000, private citizens in some instances played a crucial and "unthinkable" role in escalating or defusing the crisis.

The role of individuals, and more generally hypercomplex maps of actors in unconventional events, contribute to explaining the varied forms in which **information** can affect response efforts. Because it is produced by a vast variety of stakeholders, its sheer volume can be overwhelming; on the other hand, the heterogeneousness of these stakeholders complicates its "horizontal" and "vertical" transmission (i.e. respectively among other actors, and within hierarchical systems), leading paradoxically to a dearth of information, at least in a reliable and intelligible form. An iconic illustration of this complexity is the "ghost" of Flight American Airlines 11 on September 11, 2001, which NORAD mistakenly came to believe was headed towards Washington, when in fact it had already crashed in New York—a confusion that caused fighter jets to be scrambled after a plane that did not exist.

The problem, of course, is made even more challenging as unconventional crises systematically affect physical communication networks—most notably because of spikes in cellphone traffic—and involve a variety of responders who do not always use compatible communications and IT systems, thus forcing organizations to revert back to face-to-face contacts within and among themselves. In the wake of Hurricane Katrina, the director of New Orleans' airport insisted that first responders be based within the airport itself, even if that meant building a camp on an unused section of the tarmac, as he realized that physical proximity would be crucial to communication. On September 11, instead of blackberries or cellphones (which had failed), government officials and major corporations resorted to the services of runners to deliver messages.

A participant closely involved with response efforts on that day noted that he was away from the New York area when the attacks occurred, and had to drive back to his office, all the while unable to communicate. He eventually had to stop at a police station and use a secure phone to get in touch with colleagues and determine with them what the appropriate course of action should be. The same official, as a hurricane made landfall, described "getting calls in the middle of the night at home, from people I knew, saying the water was coming up above the second floor, at the same time that first responders were telling me that the flooding was under control. So I had to decide who to believe: and I basically went with the people who were actually getting wet, and dispatched helicopters to those sites. But they were very difficult decisions to make, the storm was going on, reports were exaggerated, I was putting first responders' lives at risk."

Lack of reliable information does not only affect leaders' awareness of how the crisis is actually unfolding: more critically, it can prevent them from forming a clear picture even of what the crisis actually *is*, or of the risks it presents. During the anthrax outbreak, U.S. officials struggled to establish the facts. As a participant put it, "it's very difficult to reassure the public when you don't know what the truth is." Specifically, initial reports claimed that anthrax had to be contracted through the skin, and could not be breathed in: this of course turned out not to be true; however, some officials shared this mistaken information with the public before it was corrected, which only deepened the crisis. In the same way, when confronting the 2003 SARS outbreak, Canadian officials initially lacked detailed information on the nature of the disease.

Both examples, in fact, point to one cause of the spread of inaccurate information in the wake of unconventional crises: namely the fact that information now can originate from every single individual, whether they are affected by the event or merely observe it. A participant recalls the degree of uncertainty that prevailed during the anthrax crisis, as ultimately unfounded reports of unidentified white powder became widespread and threatened to overwhelm authorities under a wave of false alarms and false leads. Canada was confronted to strikingly similar problems in the case of SARS—this time on a global scale.

Quality of information is also compromised when barriers among sectors, countries, or layers of decision-making prevent its effective transmission. Interconnectivity in a globalized world does not make it immune from such occurrences. In 1999, as a participant pointed out, the West Nile Virus which appeared in the U.S. was initially misidentified by the Centers for Disease Control and Prevention, in part because of insufficient communication between the veterinary and the human health systems. Similarly, China compounded the 2003 SARS crisis by keeping the initial outbreak and its scope from the international community, indeed from sections of its own government.

Even when information does cross inter-sector or other barriers, its quality can be undermined because the variety of stakeholders involved do not share the same semantics, and therefore interpret it differently. This corruption of intelligence is all the more dangerous as it is not immediately identifiable by responders. Yet, as unconventional crises come to involve ever more complex maps of actors, on an international stage, it is now crucial to highlight it, and take seriously the sociological, cultural, and linguistic issues that lay at its core.

Ultimately, however, even perfect information is not a panacea: turning it into a holy grail is both futile and misguided. As one of our participants explained, in the case of Katrina, "it wasn't a failure of information that ultimately resulted in the failure of leadership and the failure to act. Because we *had* perfect intelligence" in all respects that matter most, i.e. time, place, and "mode of attack." Therefore, it is apparent that even with perfect information, "certain conditions exist within organizations, socially, culturally, institutionally," that undermine the effectiveness of response efforts.

The make-up and structure of organizations are clearly at fault, when they are not designed to meet the threat, and prevent the organization from using its full leverage in responding to it. A participant pointed out, for instance, that 9/11 led to a reshuffling of U.S. homeland security organizations that gave excessive weight to the issue of terrorism, to the detriment of natural disasters. Katrina showed that this exclusive emphasis had been misguided. Yet Katrina also points to another cause that explains why organizations underperform in the face of unconventional events: insufficient, confusing, or unwise leadership.

A leitmotiv in the experiences recounted by our participants is the cost of lack of leadership when unconventional crises occur. Organizations have developed managerial cultures and architectures that in many respects are genuinely impressive. They combine clear guidelines for the collection and validation of data, stovepipes for their appropriate transmission, and roadmaps for rational decision-making. But catastrophic or hypercomplex events instantly overwhelm managerial logics; indeed, they thrive on their inertias and lack of vision. Effective response to those events requires leaders with unique abilities to synthesize and organize complex responses out-of-the-box. Yet, even when they exist—which is rarely the case as the selection of leaders itself is influenced by managerial paradigms—they are often stymied by the pervasive culture that surrounds them.

Our overview of catastrophic or hypercomplex crises therefore ends with a confirmation of our proposed diagnosis. Unconventional crises call for unconventional leadership.

Lessons Observed

The very repetitiveness of near-identical proposals for reform found in a litany of official reports on recent catastrophic crises shows that the phrase "lessons learned" is by itself deceptive. The same observations recur precisely because our systems have failed seriously to heed them—even in the wake of traumatic events that put these systems' deficiencies under the crudest possible light. Most of our participants in their respective fields have hit this wall of conservatism, tepidity and inertia when trying to highlight the most challenging characteristics of unconventional crises. In this context, their remarks only amount to "lessons observed."

Taken as a whole, however, they make up more than a disjointed series of warnings and diagnoses: indeed, setting up a dialogue among leaders and observers from a variety of backgrounds and sectors has allowed them to realize that their respective analyses overlap to a large extent, and at least provide as many "dots" in a coherent picture.

Four main "lessons observed," regarding the characters of unconventional crises, emerge from this picture:

- the risk posed by the "liquefaction" of systemic foundations
- the crucial role of information and knowledge
- the importance and ambiguities of leadership
- the challenges raised by allocations of tasks and coordination among sectors.

The "Liquefaction" of Systemic Foundations

The vibrations caused by earthquakes can have the peculiar effect of turning solid bodies into a state almost akin to liquid, leading to the collapse of the strongest buildings. Metaphorically, the effect of catastrophic or hypercomplex events on our systems is similar—their best lines of defense fail to protect them effectively as their very foundations are undermined, made irrelevant, or indeed turned into a liability.

In unconventional crises, "liquefaction" first and foremost affects **"foundational paradigms"**: the assumptions on which our systems are based, because they underlie perceptions of their identity, purpose, and presumed strength. As a participant put it, "crises often involve paradigm shifts which leaders do not immediately detect. The world has changed around them: and while they are fighting the last war, the next war occurs on a different planet, and they're not there with it."

On September 11, 2001, NORAD, as well as military guidelines for response to airborne threats and hijackings, were still geared toward a confrontation with the Soviet Union and "conventional" terrorists. Similarly, during the fuel protests that affected the UK in 2000, members of the British government for a long time could not bring themselves to realize, or believe, just how vulnerable the country's economy was to disruptions in the fuel supply network.

Threats to foundational paradigms are especially difficult to identify in a timely fashion because leaders often will be culturally unwilling to heed warnings about them, as they find their implications too disturbing to contemplate. This is the root of the "failure of imagination" that the 9/11 Commission and other after-event reports highlighted. For instance, in 2000, when news first arose of projected blockades around refineries, oil companies tried to warn the British government about the potential disruptions that could follow: they were met with disbelief.

Past the initial phase when bad news is simply ignored, the "Titanic" syndrome lives on, as leaders abandon the comfort of their foundational paradigms (the "invulnerability of the ship") only reluctantly. First, they tend to demand an overwhelming body of incontrovertible evidence before accepting that the paradigm has been breached—all the while making ill-conceived decisions, which can prove fatal in unconventional environments when timeliness is of the essence. In addition, the dissemination of such evidence stutters through the levels of bureaucratic communication channels, as disbelief adds to disbelief, and each echelon eschews the responsibility of being the harbinger of bad news.

In addition to intangible "paradigms," our systems are based on relationships of "hard" and "soft" power. With respect to the former, a systemic hierarchy is premised on the fact that a higher rank within it entails a greater capacity to impact lower-level actors through one's decisions, and to remain immune from the decisions of subordinates. However, unconventional events challenge this most basic axiom on which our systems are premised, threatening the validity of the notion of "power" altogether.

In the specific "unconventional" case of the challenge posed to traditional militaries by guerrilla tactics or terrorism, this paradigm-shifting collapse of power has been characterized as "**asymmetric**": but the word holds true in a more general context.

In our complex, inter-dependent, "just-in-time" systems, asymmetric power derives most often from the capacity of groups (or even individuals) to gain control of crucial hubs in the network. This was made clear for instance during the 2000 fuel protests in the U.K., when a small number of truck drivers and farmers applied a critical pinch on a crucial and highly vulnerable hub in the British economic system—refineries.

In such circumstances, when traditional leaders are threatened by an "angry mob," they tend to take refuge in haughty positions of power built into normal hierarchical systems, a "situation room," in the hope to organize the seemingly inevitable crushing of the "peasants' revolt" from their modern-day dungeon. In fact, this move usually proves counter-productive, or indeed fatal, as it fails to take into account that the definition of "power" has shifted to make the "dungeon" irrelevant, and has turned it into a self-inflicted prison. "In a secure crisis room twenty-five feet below Whitehall, there's nothing you can do about people who want to buy petrol in North-West England." For leaders, what does "power" mean when their decisions have less impact on a handful of citizens than the latter's have on government? Again, in 2000, the fuel protests not only shook the British economy to its core: they also forced Downing Street and Whitehall into near-complete powerlessness, in a matter of days.

The liquefaction of "power" has an important knock-on effect: it causes systems based upon it to disintegrate into ad hoc sub-units that define new solidarities, interests, and self-preservation instincts. Stunned by the first occurrence of an unconventional crisis, leaders all too often overlook this point, and fail to realize that solidarities vis-à-vis the State, the community at large, etc. in fact are no longer priorities for those affected by or involved in the event, as sub-units like local communities, families, or even self, have become the dominant terms of reference. In 2000, in a desperate attempt to recover some degree of control over the public's behavior, the British Prime Minister warned that fuel protests "would cost the government millions." As a participant noted, however, "no one cares if something costs the government millions—it doesn't relate to normal experience." On the other hand, where the Prime Minister had failed, a private citizen succeeded by confronting strikers while TV crews were filming, and making the point that their blockades compromised the capacity of hospitals to treat *their* relatives. "And that—that turned it. Suddenly people got wind of something that related to *them*."

Beyond "hard power," i.e. the capacity of one's decisions to affect the behaviors and choices of others, systems are also built upon a foundation of "soft power"—in the first place, **trust**. When all else has failed, trust can be the only glue that keeps a system coherent and self-conscious enough to be capable of working toward its own self-preservation. Conversely, in the wake of unconventional events, loss of trust can be the last straw, the coup-de-grâce for a weakened system, "when actors become so lacking in confidence, they just decide to take control of their own destinies."

This intangible underwriter of social contracts is borne out of the fulfillment of expectations. Therefore, in unconventional situations, it is most often compromised for two different reasons: either because leaders struggle to accomplish their mission, or because the public's expectations of them are excessive.

The "stun effect" that unconventional events often cause among leadership structures is especially problematic because it compromises *from the very start* the public's trust in their leaders' competence, commitment and courage. Poor communication, brought out in part by excessive reliance on traditional "crisis management" spin, only compounds the problem: especially when, based on a mistaken obsession with "reassuring the public," leaders understate the challenges at stake. During the 2000 fuel crisis, after just such a "reassuring" message from the British Prime Minister, "the public started to believe the crisis would actually be over in twenty-four hours. Twenty-four hours later, when it clearly was not, trust in the government's word went out the window."

On the other hand, a number of participants noted that in Western polities at least, public expectations of their governments are often unrealistic when catastrophic crises hit, and through their sheer scale prevent leaders and responders from rescuing all victims rapidly. Our polities cannot long be subjected to repeated deleterious collapses of trust caused by excessive expectations. As we explain in more details below, the solution must be a heightened effort to educate the public about the implications of catastrophic events, ensure better preparedness from individuals and local communities alike, and turn the call for "72-hour self-reliance" from an empty slogan into a building block of our democratic contracts.

The Crucial Role of Information and Knowledge

In addition to "trust," soft power within systems also derives from the capacity of those higher up the hierarchical ladder to collect more complete or accurate information. Yet this is also threatened by unconventional events, which compounds the loss of substance of traditional power structures.

As we have seen, catastrophic or hypercomplex crises create a confusing kaleidoscope of facts, which challenges the capacity of leaders to collect complete and accurate information or make sense of it. In an environment where asymmetric power rules, and groups' or even individuals' decision can have significant impacts on the course of events, information is produced from a bewildering variety of sources, and with extreme granularity.

Leadership structures such as governments are often equipped to construct centralized assessments at the "macro" levels, but can be poorly attuned to micro situations "on the ground," and struggle to create a coherent and actionable picture out of local data. Communications between the "center" and unconventional local relays, capable of sensing such intangibles as the mood of local populations, the media, or interest groups, prove invaluable for leadership structures in such circumstances: but they often are not formally included in official hierarchical charts, and centralized information-management bureaucracies.

In addition, **contacts between the Center and local actors** must work along "two-way" channels, and to the benefit of both, rather than be driven by the upper echelon's misplaced and ultimately futile obsession with the mantra of "situational awareness." A participant from the private sector characterized the government's thirst for exhaustive information, and its unwelcome effects, in the following terms: "[In essence, they would tell us:] 'We don't want to be there, and in fact we are not there, but can you tell us everything you know?' —It just doesn't work that way! We found that it was far more effective when we could engage in information-sharing for direct and mutual benefit: 'Here is what I need to know: what is the perimeter zone? How do I get employees in to do assessments? How do I take that information and then funnel it back to you in a useful way?' When we had points of contact [in government] that were willing to respond and think the issue through, *that's* information sharing, *that's* a value to the actual responders."

Thorough information-sharing with responders on the ground must be combined with a capacity to produce a single assessment—an agreed set of facts which "enables decision-makers to focus on making decisions, rather than arguing over semantics." In the case of the 2000 UK fuel protests, these joint assessments were prepared by a team that combined civil servants, trade unionists, press officers, oil company executives, and policemen. In the aftermath of Hurricane Katrina, a communication company opened up its emergency response center to all of its counterparts—wireless, wireline, cable—and enabled the sector as a whole to develop common assessments and priorities. Twice a day, in the first two weeks following landfall, all seventeen major critical infrastructure sectors held conference calls, sharing status: "Out of that, we developed a situational awareness picture that was then sent to Homeland Security"—although it sometimes found itself strangely distorted and muddled once it got there... At New Orleans Airport, which became simultaneously the main airport in the country, a hospital, a dormitory, and a morgue in the days after the storm, the Director of Aviation set up no fewer than four command posts, respectively for the "normal" leadership of the airport, the military, and medical staff—while the fourth provided a single meeting point where all of the actors involved would meet daily to make decisions and assess the situation in common.

The considerable inertia of bureaucratic, hierarchical, and **stovepiped organizations** geared toward the management of "normal" events systematically impedes efforts to set up such ad hoc mechanisms for inclusive communication and shared assessment in a timely and coherent fashion. As a participant pointed out, by September 11, 2001, "The military and Federal Aviation Authority, which initially had joint control of the U.S. airspace, had evolved into different silos. The FAA had gained supremacy. Over time, they evolved separate ways of doing business; they had separate vocabularies; their radars didn't line up: they didn't look at the same picture." In New York, meanwhile, it is well documented that historical rivalries between the Fire Department and Police prevented them from seriously talking to each other as the crisis unfolded, a problem which technical difficulties merely compounded.

Of course, the difficulty of producing shared assessments is also heightened by technical challenges, when leaders and responders are not physically in contact with one another, and must develop "virtual platforms." This holds true especially in hypercomplex events that involve a variety of actors, each likely to use a different IT system for collecting and interpreting data. The response to the 2005 earthquake in Kashmir was a case in point, as the many NGOs involved found themselves without a common IT platform.

Hierarchical architectures can be just as much of a liability as physical or virtual stovepipes: on September 11, 2001, "when a controller heard indication that there was a hijacking, the information was supposed to go up the chain: in other words from the controller, to his supervisor, to the region, to the FAA command center at Herndon, to FAA headquarters in Washington: once it got there, they would call the Secretary of Defense, and it would work its way back down the military chain until finally fighters would be scrambled. Well, *that* didn't work on 9/11. In fact, after the second plane, *nobody even really tried to make that work*. So, the Air National Guard folks and the controllers were basically improvising." Similarly, during the 2003 SARS outbreak in Toronto, when a doctor found that a patient might have the disease, "the doctor told the hospital administration, the hospital administration called Toronto Public Health, which called the Province of Ontario, which told Health Canada, which told the World Health Organization. The WHO had a question: they asked Health Canada, Health Canada asked Ontario, Ontario asked Toronto, Toronto phoned the hospital, eventually the doctor gave the answer, and back up the stream it went: that's two or three days that had gone by, and since in the meantime each 'link' in the chain had been giving press conferences, they appeared not to be in synch—because they weren't."

In any case, when unconventional events strike, the most crucial challenge for leaders is not so much to rebuild effective information systems, but rather to recognize that perfect information cannot be this time a source of power, as it is unattainable: and that they must **act without it**.

Issues arising from the *collection* of information are compounded by the fact that leaders now have lost their traditional monopoly on its *diffusion*. During the 2000 protests in the UK, fuel happened to be the ad hoc critical hub that enabled individuals or groups to yield asymmetric power: but the media play such a role in *all* unconventional crises. As a participant put it, "on a Sunday, a single individual emptied the West of England of petrol," simply by informing the media that protesters would blockade a local refinery the next day, which caused the general public to stock up on fuel and empty local gas stations in twenty-four hours—*without* a single picket actually occurring.

Even assuming that information is collected and disseminated, unconventional events make its *interpretation*, i.e. its conversion into actionable knowledge, more difficult than it would appear at first glance. Indeed, the complexity of these crises compromises the validity of intellectual mechanisms that have traditionally enabled leaders and public alike to sift through information and determine which should be trusted enough to be the basis for action. Our "post-positivist" societies used to endow science with this role: yet in the face of hypercomplexity, **over-reliance on scientific reasoning** can in fact turn into a liability. As a participant pointed out, the World Health Organization's decision to issue a travel advisory against the Toronto area following the SARS outbreak in the city in 2003 may have been based on sound science (though even this is debatable): but by failing to take into account the economic and societal repercussions of this decision, the WHO turned its reliance on scientific knowledge into part of the problem, rather than of the solution. In case of a flu pandemic outbreak, an attempt to close borders or impose quarantines in the name of science would exhibit the same basic flaws, and lead to similarly catastrophic consequences: these measures would not in fact stop the disease, but would have incalculably disruptive and costly knock-on effects, all the while diverting precious resources; most importantly, they would inevitably cause an irreversible loss of public trust once they failed.

The problem is compounded by the fact that leaders destabilized by unconventional or "unthinkable" events, and eager to be seen as "doing something," will grab to "what they know" (or what they think they know) for dear life, and rush with delight to comfort zones where black-and-white still prevails. Culturally, "science," or the appearance of it, is one such island of certainty in worlds gone mad. The irresistible draw of the "scientific mirage" will adversely affect decision-making in two ways: first, it will cause leaders to set their course of action based on science that in fact is not sufficiently mature to provide trustworthy bearings. Thus, calls for the public to wear special N95 masks during SARS turned out to *not* to be warranted (and indeed, to increase the risks incurred) once further scientific research into their effectiveness had been conducted.

Second, as in the case of the WHO's travel advisory, leaders' exclusive focus on the beacon of science threatens to hypnotize them and make them lose their peripheral vision, that is, their awareness of interdependencies and cascading effects that may come back to haunt them. As a participant put it, when advising his political hierarchy against the temptation of basing their decisions exclusively on science, he was in effect "trying to save them from themselves."

If leaders think through the potentially disruptive knock-on effects of such initiatives, and decide against making science the only determinant of the wisdom of policy options, it is then incumbent upon them to educate the public about their conclusions and the analytical process behind them. This is because the greater public, in the highly confusing environment brought about by unconventional events, will be equally fascinated by the apparent certainty that science provides—and even less likely to distinguish proven from unsound assertions. If leaders make decisions that seemingly run counter to what science (or pseudo-science) call for, the loss of public trust that ensues can be immediate and irreparable. As a participant explained, "if public health authorities decide *not* to use antivirals such as Tamiflu for prophylaxis in advance of a pandemic—based on the fact that this would reduce their effectiveness as a treatment—the key then becomes educating the public in advance, so they recognize that not everyone should be expecting to get them, and they understand why."

On the whole, therefore, the challenges posed by the collection, interpretation, and dissemination of information in catastrophic or hypercomplex events far transcend the old techniques of media-savvy "crisis information-management." It is all the more concerning that leaders often think themselves sufficiently prepared when they have mastered these skills, or outsourced them to a praetorian guard of spin-doctors.

The Importance and Ambiguities of Leadership

The liquefaction of systemic foundations provoked by catastrophic events does not entail the irrelevance of leadership. On the contrary, it makes it more important than ever—if leadership manages to become just as unconventional as the event it is called upon to confront. Rebuilding a system ad-hoc when its lines of defense have been breached, or making sense of complex and confusing information, can only be achieved through coherent, credible, and determined leadership. As noted above, managerial techniques or bureaucratic firewalls fall short of the mark when it comes to dealing with unconventional events, and might indeed turn into fatal liabilities.

In the words of a participant, "the same people at FEMA who were criticized terribly for their response to Hurricane Andrew in 1992 were praised for successfully responding to Midwest floods, the Oklahoma City bombing, September 11. What was the difference? It's the leadership that made the bureaucracy function." Throughout the confusion of September 11, 2001, the Northeast Air Defense Sector only retained some clarity of vision and unity of purpose because of the leadership of its commanding officer—who stayed in a back room, listening to the bewildering conversations between his team, NORAD headquarters, and the FAA, one step removed from the crisis, and only intervened when the urgency of the operational response threatened to cause decisions that went against broader strategic imperatives.

While in universal agreement on this point, our participants highlighted three crucial caveats. First, the unconventional nature of leadership needed to prepare for and respond to catastrophic or hypercomplex events means that "de facto" leaders might not turn out to be those whom normal hierarchical charts identify as such. For instance, "by the time the President and the Vice-President got engaged on 9/11, the crisis was over! The shoot-down order came down at 10:31 a.m.—almost a half hour after the last plane had crashed in Pennsylvania." Operational officers at NORAD, or mid-level New York City firefighters and policemen, had more influence on the events of that day than the upper echelons of the Federal government. During the 2000 fuel protests, local British police managed to negotiate temporary lifts of the refineries' blockades with protesters in order to allow for the delivery of critical fuel supplies e.g. to hospitals. "The ministers saw this on television, and went ballistic: not least because it showed who was in charge—and it was certainly not the government."

In this context, in fact, the actions of "theoretical" leaders, and their efforts to recover their "natural" position against the claims of those that emerge ad hoc on the ground, might actually impede response efforts. A participant involved in recovery efforts in the wake of Hurricane Katrina recalled that Washington's obsession with "situational awareness" compelled many responders to devote time that they did not possess in order to provide the required information. Similarly, diplomats or humanitarian officials noted that their superiors' eagerness to appear as "doing something" on the ground, for political reasons far removed from the internal dynamics of the crisis, actually compounded the difficulty of practical recovery efforts—even though it could on occasion bestow welcome visibility on the crisis they had to confront.

Finally, in the aftermath of unconventional events, "normal" leaders, as well as those who are "crowned kings" by circumstances, must not simply replicate pre-existing centralized arrangements: but rather accept, against the grain of prevalent culture, the need for such empowerment as will enable risk-taking from responders on the ground at every level. Unconventional events make empowerment of local actors critical because they compromise system-wide communications, and thereby restrict the framework of decision making and *trust* to face-to-face contacts.

Here again, simply bandying about the mantra of "empowerment" falls far short of the mark. What is needed is a reform of leadership *culture* that will remove the many obstacles that currently impede any delegation of authority other than cosmetic: such as issues of legal responsibility or, more generally, a culture in which organizations cannot be trusted to support and shield a leader who does decide to empower his or her subordinates, if and when things go wrong.

These conclusions hold a crucial lesson for planning efforts: plans which assume, as most unfortunately do, that "pre-crisis" leadership not only will *survive* an unconventional event, but will retain its exclusively dominant position through it, are often condemned to immediate irrelevancy in its wake. Planners would be better advised to anticipate a context in which ad hoc leaders will emerge from a variety of sources (even the most unsuspected), and will be forced genuinely to delegate decision-making powers to responders on the ground. Clearly this represents a fundamental challenge to cultural paradigms of traditional planning efforts—and even a challenge to what planning is *for*, since plans all too often aim less genuinely to prepare for potential events, than to reinforce "normal" leaders' claim to supremacy here and now, by making the symbolic case that their powers *will* remain intact in all circumstances, however catastrophic and unconventional.

The Challenges of Inter-Sector Coordination

On both sides of the Atlantic (most visibly in some European countries), the public sector has enjoyed a traditional monopoly on crisis planning and response. This is because governments for long were alone in combining national reach, international leverage, and military capabilities. Indeed, the public sector often founded its identity upon its primacy in these various respects.

Today, however, all of these monopolies are being contested. Major companies and NGOs now exert significant influence nationally; in a globalized world, they have woven dense webs of transnational partnerships; and, through the hiring of private military companies or other means, they are even challenging the State's Weberian "monopoly on legitimate violence."

This raises major questions of democratic accountability, as unelected and politically irresponsible actors take on vast swaths of civic responsibilities that traditionally had been the preserve of governments. The arcane backgrounds and agendas of some NGOs are being called into question with increasing frequency as they garner significant influence—but the power yielded by major companies can be equally problematic in crisis situations if the public sector fails to ensure that it is *built into a new Social Contract* in which the public's interest and the public's voice remain paramount.

In the wake of catastrophic events that shed a glaring light on their strategic and operational deficiencies, governments now increasingly call for corporate and humanitarian partners to take up some of the burden in response efforts: this most notably has been the case in the United States, following the trauma of Hurricane Katrina.

However, the bargain can only hold if the underlying culture changes with the allocation of tasks: and that, noticeably, has not been the case. Even in fields over which it conspicuously has limited control, such as the Internet, the public sector continues to perceive itself as the "natural" and indeed exclusive leader of planning and response efforts. It still constrains their organization within a set of excessively rigid rules and regulations.

In a U.S. context, as one participant noted, the National Response Plan purports to specify not only the course of action expected from private and humanitarian partners (thus exhibiting all the weaknesses of "behavioral plans" described later in this report), but also *who* should be considered a partner in the first place, through the mechanism of Emergency Support Functions (ESF). Companies that are not clearly included in the ESF structure find themselves in a frustrating limbo. This is all the more regrettable as the reason for their exclusion from the framework usually is that they are emerging companies in newer fields of activity, which often could make significant and unforeseen contributions to response efforts.

The Stafford Act also constrains the margin of maneuver of non-governmental partners in ways that can compromise their effectiveness—even though their restoration efforts can be vital to those of the public sector itself. As a participant recalled, the response from critical infrastructure providers after Katrina was often hampered by a provision in the Act that prevents government from conferring a direct benefit on the private sector—which most notably precluded the military from providing security to private companies. In addition, the Act merely represents the "tip of the iceberg," as the U.S. system confronts private and humanitarian responders with layer upon layer of laws and regulation, from local to Federal level. Legalistic impediments to mutual inter-sector cooperation are especially problematic when they prevent non-governmental actors from even *reaching* an impacted zone, because of restrictions imposed by the military.

More generally, in the absence of genuine trust and a balanced contract between government and other sectors, the latter (especially the corporate world) inevitably remain hesitant to share information or combine operational efforts, as they can never be certain that the public sector will not divulge that information to their detriment, or "commandeer" their operational resources to sustain its own response.

Faced with these impasses, non-governmental partners have laid out ad hoc "parallel" platforms for information-sharing and cooperation —what a participant described as "self-organizing mechanisms within spontaneous communities." For all their effectiveness, it remains unacceptable that the public sector, through its overly exclusive leadership culture, should cause such ad hoc arrangements to grow outside of (indeed in opposition to) government planning and coordination, in a limbo of democratic unaccountability. The way out of this dilemma is simple: the public sector must accept to share strategic leadership in addition to operational responsibilities.

Certainly coordination among various sectors is possible. Significant improvements have often been made in this respect following the trauma of catastrophic crises. For instance, public-private cooperation in New York on 9/11 proved remarkably effective in large part because of the lessons learned from the 1993 bombing of the World Trade Center, and planning efforts undertaken by all stakeholders in anticipation of Millenium-related crises such as Y2K.

However, the example of New York City does not have universal value, as it is circumscribed in scope to a single city—however vast. In larger and more complex contexts, which involve a much greater variety of stakeholders—including on an international scale—coordination must prove a much more difficult proposition. Although it seems to entail a rough equality of status among actors, "coordination" in actual fact can only mean that one among them carves out the others' respective areas of competence, and determines their missions in order to avoid overlap and redundancy. When dealing with a bewildering number of international stakeholders, whose identity and motivations are obscure to one another, this is a very difficult expectation indeed.

One of our participants, therefore, argues for the concept of *alignment*, instead of *coordination*: this means that, when responding to complex events involving a multiplicity of actors, the priority must be, through information-sharing, to ensure that they share a common purpose, and a single broad strategy, so that their respective efforts can complement and strengthen one another.

The Way Forward

"Lessons observed" can only turn into "lessons learned" if the analysis that our participants proposed can lead to concrete reforms, in Europe as well as North America. The first phase of our project, in 2006-2007, aimed to lay out a common framework of analysis, even common semantics, among leaders and specialists that have had to confront unconventional events, irrespective of country and sector. This was achieved with remarkable success.

Based on this "toolbox," we then launched the second phase of the project, aiming to develop concrete proposals for change.

We have laid out five main strategic frameworks in which reform can, and indeed must, take place. Simply put, confronting unconventional crises requires that we modify:

- most fundamentally, the make-up of our systems

- the "Social Contract" of inter-sector allocation of tasks

- the underlying logic and goal of our planning efforts

- the mechanism and philosophy of crisis management response

- the generational transmission of knowledge and culture through the education of future leaders.

Building Response Mechanisms Into "Normal" Systems

Conventional crises rarely require high levels of inbuilt resiliency from our systems. This is because such events tend to affect circumscribed "ground zeros," and therefore can be tackled by bringing to bear the "normal" assets and strategies of the unscathed outside on the impacted area.

On the other hand, catastrophic or hypercomplex events will destabilize entire systems, forcing leaders and public alike to abandon "normality" altogether, and look for a coherent fallback position. However, it is eminently difficult to organize an orderly general retreat, especially when leaders must redefine a new line of defense while on the run, and from the ground up. Miracles at Dunkirk are precisely that: miracles.

Even before the planning phase, and more fundamentally, the makeup of our systems itself must anticipate the destabilizing effects of unconventional events by weaving resiliencies (visible or "hidden") into their fabric. For instance, following 9/11 and Hurricane Katrina, many companies in the financial or communications sectors, as well as NGOs, have rebuilt their systems to include back-up command-and-control centers separated by virtual or physical firewalls (most simply, geographical distance between various critical sites) in order to ensure continuity of effort in the event that their headquarters themselves are destroyed by a catastrophic event, or multiple sites are needed to respond to it.

To the extent possible, this must be done in such a way that these resiliencies, as they are built into normal systems, will benefit their "routine" effectiveness, and not provoke excessive additional costs. However, even if strengthening our systems does prove costly, expenses incurred in the process will pale in comparison to the cost of rebuilding them from the ground up, when their lack of resiliency has enabled catastrophic events to annihilate them.

This concerns the strategic as well as the operational level: in other words, our "normal" systems should be underpinned not only by latent alternative resources, but by alternative allocations of civic responsibility. For instance, in private companies best prepared to confront hurricanes, employees are dual-hatted year-round: in addition to their "normal" job, they are attributed a secondary role in case of a major disaster—be it allocating or restoring assets, or taking charge of the welfare of employees' families—and continuously train for it.

Another characteristic of unconventional events makes it essential that our systems can rely on inbuilt resiliencies, and thereby retain their strategic and operational "spine" even when hit by a crisis. Generally speaking, "normal" crises follow a neat pattern in which "normal status" is followed by crisis, response, and recovery. In each phase, a specific agent takes the lead, and withdraws when its task is complete—without much concern for the working conditions that it leaves behind to its successor, as it trusts that in any case they will not be excessively far removed from "normality." On the other hand, catastrophic or hypercomplex events do not lend themselves to this clear succession of phases. The choices made by initial responders, when called upon to redefine goals and strategies, will affect (and indeed can compromise) the effectiveness of long-term reconstruction efforts, because the two are inextricably linked. Responders themselves, incidentally, will often be unable to withdraw and transition to a different leadership, but will have to stay on and contribute to reconstruction. However, given the time pressures that affect their work, they cannot be expected unfailingly to define strategies and mechanisms that will remain valid and helpful in later stages, if they must do so without any systemic foundations or guidelines. Resiliencies built into our systems provide just such foundations.

A New Social Contract:
Redrawing Inter-Sector Allocations of Tasks

As we have seen, the public sector, for deeply ingrained cultural reasons, tends to restrict the margin of maneuver of non-governmental actors' through plans, rules and regulations, even as it asks them to take on increased responsibility for response efforts. The solution to this quandary is not to abandon plans, rules and regulations, but for government genuinely to invite its counterparts to the table so they can share in the process of drawing them up, thus turning them into actual "partners" beyond tired slogans. In various contexts, this means that governments must accept the *"révision déchirante"* not only of *testing* the next NRP or Plan ORSEC by submitting it to the private sector once it is drafted, but of *co-authoring* it with them.

In July 2004, a number of emergency management professionals famously organized the "Hurricane Pam" exercise, which provided daunting glimpses of the havoc Katrina would wreak on the Gulf Coast little more than a year later: yet it is telling that representatives from the private sector simply were not invited to take part. None of the organizers and participants at the time seem to have given more than a passing thought to this glaring omission. This incident perfectly encapsulates the fallacies of the "public-private partnership" mantra, and the need for a fundamental cultural shift in this respect.

Response efforts must also exhibit the same openness: in other words, private and humanitarian actors must be included within government's crisis cells (such as FEMA's joint field offices), at the top of the "information ladder," and must take part in the definition of strategic outlooks and priorities, as well as the elaboration of common situational assessments.

This inclusiveness must not be restricted to sections of the private or humanitarian sectors with which government has had long-standing working relationships. From the perspective of these well-identified partners, e.g. communication or financial services in the U.S., frameworks such as the National Response Plan and Emergency Support Functions certainly have been useful in enabling policy coordination among themselves and with government: but that does not hold true of emerging, "new technology" sectors, or small businesses.

Drawing a new social contract is the only way effectively to tackle a major problem in crisis planning: the prioritization of response efforts. As long as the determination of priorities is perceived to be exclusively in the hands of government, it will be subject to the suspicions of all other stakeholders. Prioritization inevitably creates losers and winners, and the sacrifices this entails can only be borne if all stakeholders trust that their voice has been heard in the process. Otherwise, reluctance and recriminations will be such that theoretical lists of priorities are doomed to irrelevancy in the wake of a crisis. More to the point, awareness of this fact all to often leads government to avoid tackling the issue of prioritization altogether; misguided and over-hasty reconstruction efforts on the Gulf Coast shed a crude and depressing light on the dangers incurred by eschewing the issue.

The challenge involved in the redrawing of allocation of tasks is fundamentally cultural, and so is the solution to it. As a participant mentioned, "too often it seems as though bureaucracies exist primarily to deflect blame, rather than to solve problems. They may not start that way but they evolve that way. A solution might be to change the system's incentives, in other words the definition of success in our organizations. If you define success in a quantifiable way as 'cooperating with other bureaucracies', it might be a first step in avoiding the 'silo' effect that plagued the U.S. from top to bottom on September 11."

Beyond public, private, or humanitarian organizations and bureaucracies, the redrawing of "Social Contracts" must include "civic" actors and the greater public at large. Fundamentally, a new contract is necessary because our democracies cannot long endure to be hit time and again by catastrophic event that ruin the illusion of public sector omnipotence, and public trust in their elected leaders: therefore, for the sake of our systems' permanence, a greater role must be given to the general public.

In addition, a grand bargain that bestows more responsibility on the public, while giving it more say in planning and response efforts at the highest level, also makes sense for purely practical, operational reasons. All Western polities (but especially the United States, with its tradition of individual self-reliance and limited government control), when facing the prospect of catastrophic events, can ill afford to forego the incalculable contribution that the public can make—*if properly prepared* through individual and "micro-level" preparedness programs, and if government balances its calls for increased self-reliance with genuine empowerment and an invitation for civil society to sit at the table when plans are drawn and response strategies are prepared.

This foremost aspect in the needed revision of Social Contracts is also the most challenging to prevalent public sector culture. Opening up leadership, preparedness, and response efforts to the greater public means that government must turn emergency preparedness and homeland security into genuinely democratic, collective endeavors, and back away from its futile attempt to preserve its monopoly on these issues (or even, it seems, the mystique of its efforts) by placing them beyond a forbidding barrier of security clearances and technical jargon. The ill-thought "color-coded threat system," which purports to engage the public but stops halfway in the process—and before it makes any sense—would be an amusing case in point if it was not so deadly serious.

From "Behavioral" to Resource-Based Planning

In the face of catastrophic or hypercomplex crises, **behavioral planning**—that is, planning that focuses on prescribing courses of action to follow in specific circumstances—is bound to fail, and indeed to turn into part of the problem rather than of the solution, for several reasons:

First and foremost, it compounds the "stun effect" that catastrophic crises tend to provoke when they go beyond anticipated scenarios. Panic arises when leaders (and members of the public) are armed only with prescriptions based on assumptions that a hypercomplex crisis makes instantly obsolete. Further, a culture of behavioral plans reinforces the tendency of leaders to refuse to anticipate the "unthinkable," as they sense that it threatens the validity of pre-defined courses of action.

This concerns more than the operational level. On a strategic plane, the legitimacy of hierarchies, as well as leaders' individual identities, are unfortunately founded on *what leaders do*. A crisis that prevents them from following prescribed behaviors will therefore compound its destabilizing effects on systems of decision and action by putting into question the leaders' capacity to act, hence their self-perception as well as the public's perception of them. This will inevitably compound stun effects, and (through the loss of trust and the collapse of hierarchical architectures) lead to the "liquefaction of social contracts" among and between the greater public and leaders.

Third, the course of action prescribed by a "behavioral" plan for one set of actors does not make sense (and indeed is not practicable) in isolation, but only as part of a "behavioral chain," which proverbially is only as strong as its weakest link: in other words, if lack of resources (most notably communications), confusion, or even death or injury make it impossible for one actor to behave in the way called for by the plan, this often has the cascading effect of preventing other stakeholders to follow the course of action required by the plan in their own case. This in fact is a vicious circle, as incapacity to act efficiently or to act at all, as we have just seen, will compromise the integrity of hierarchical systems, and thereby weaken at once the entire "chain of behaviors" anticipated in the plans.

Fourth, behavior-based planning assumes that pre-event rationality will still apply after the crisis hits. This, unfortunately, often turns out not to be the case. Again, catastrophic or hypercomplex crises destabilize entire systems, and a decision's rationality is only defined against the backdrop of the system or context in which it is made. In the case of Hurricane Katrina, courses of action that might have seemed entirely rational and reasonable before the storm became counterproductive in its wake. Plans should not prescribe rationality, but put actors in a position to *redefine what rationality means* in post-crisis circumstances.

Fifth, since each type of crisis corresponds to a set course of actions (although basic behavioral prescriptions might sometimes converge irrespective of the specific crisis at hand), behavior-based planning tends to take as its starting point an ever-expanding spectrum of potential events. This is inefficient and ultimately futile, as hypercomplex crises will not conform to any such predetermined scenario. The aim to anticipate all potential hazards is bound to compound "stun effects" in the aftermath of unconventional crises, as leaders realize that actual events do not in fact resemble any of the scenarios envisaged in their plans. As many analysts observed in the wake of hurricane Katrina, effective response should not wait until we are hit by the crises that we have prepared for.

More fundamentally, behavioral planning fails because it assumes wrongly (in the case of catastrophic crises) that what will matter most will be the leaders' behavior: that they will call the shots, and fight the crisis on their own terrain, so that their decisions can circumscribe, reduce, and ultimately resolve the crisis. This perspective is mistaken. Following Hurricane Katrina, the leadership of New Orleans Airport suddenly found that its old turf had been turned overnight into a military base, a hospital, and a campground for victims and first responders, among other things. In addition, as the director noted: "We normally only had commercial passenger airplanes: but in the days following the hurricane, we had thirty or forty helicopters at a time bringing in people that had been rescued from trees or rooftops. No one would ever want that circumstance. Going 'by the book', you would say that's unacceptably dangerous: but we had no choice! These people were going to come in whether we liked it or not."

In other words, catastrophic crises, physically and in systemic terms, will make the "playing field" unrecognizable. They will impose *their* rules, their pitfalls. What matters most will be *their* behavior. Leaders and the greater public will not be able to act from the comfort of a "safe outside," a General HQ removed from the battlefield. Even in what used to be their own turf, they will find themselves, in essence, behind enemy lines.

This last metaphor is especially useful, as it points us towards the doctrine of military special forces, which holds many relevant lessons. For special forces, plans that would presume to set specific courses of action in every single possible contingency would amount to suicide. So would plans based on hierarchical constructs where actors' identities, and their relationships to others, would be described and circumscribed by their capacity to act "in the way they are supposed to." Unique in the military, they are trained not to be stunned by unpredictability, but to thrive on it. That is because they rely not on behavioral, but on resource-based plans.

Behind enemy lines, in an environment where "the crisis calls the shots," resources are scarce, the environment is hostile, outside help is out of the question, and rationality needs to be reinvented, what is needed from a plan is a **description of the building blocks** that will enable actors to redefine by and for themselves the appropriate course of action. Again, the special forces metaphor is useful. Their survival courses start from the premise that basic resources that underpin "normal" systems will no longer be available: they then go through a list of such "missing resources," and for each describe an "ersatz," an alternate resource. Depending on the exact situation—which instructors do not claim to anticipate exactly—these alternate resources through *innovation and ingenuity* (stifled by behavioral plans) can then be combined to recreate a rational system. Alternate resources will suggest the appropriate course of action: behavior will be defined by resources.

Trusting that actors, in the face of a catastrophic or hypercomplex crisis, can be similarly self-reliant in redefining their own course of action if given a "toolbox" of potential alternate resources is by no means an overambitious goal—not only for leaders, but for the greater public as well.

"Panic," to a large extent, is a myth. Plans that describe set courses of actions will lead to panic because, as soon as actors realize that the emerging event does not conform to any envisaged scenario, and makes it impossible for them to adopt the prescribed course of action, they at once lose their bearings, their place in the hierarchical architecture, and their capacity to make sense of events. Ironically, the drafters of behavioral plans tend to believe that developing more such plans in more intricate details is the only way to prevent the "natural reaction" that is panic, when in actual facts panic is *caused* by the limits of these very plans.

Panic reactions are not nearly as "natural" as is commonly thought. Faced with an unconventional event, people can, indeed will remain rational if given the proper "building blocks" to recover their bearings. Indeed catastrophic crises provoke supremely rational decisions, as the spectrum of priorities and choices suddenly shrinks to basic matters of life and death.

Based on this premise, what is needed is the development of generic plans that do not claim to anticipate the exact details of each potential emergent event, and do not *a priori* prescribe behaviors, but help the victims of catastrophic crises (who more likely than not *will* include first responders) to **identify alternate resources**.

For instance, leaders and the wider public would have been much better off after Katrina if plans had not described courses of action that turned out to be entirely impractical, and indeed counter-productive —but had signaled, and made available, alternate modes of support. They could have explained that text messages would be the last mode of communication available when all else had failed. Before the storm, sensing that warning messages broadcast on television and radio were insufficient, Governor Blanco of Louisiana thought of contacting clergy throughout the state to urge them to reiterate the message to their congregations (the storm hit on a Sunday night): this type of out-of-the-box alternate resources should not have been left to intuition, but "flagged" ahead of time.

Loss of basic resources is an excellent entry point for planning efforts because it is the one unavoidable and common effect of *all* catastrophic crises, whatever their exact type: so that anticipating this loss enables plans to remain generic, and universally applicable. What is to be done when power is lost? When communications are lost? When the trust of the public is lost? When leaders themselves are victims— unavailable, powerless, or dead? These are the terms that catastrophic crisis will *impose*: these are the terms to which (or under which) we should be prepared to respond. Granted, in some cases, no alternate resource will exist: but at least we will have identified the vulnerabilities that are genuinely crucial in our initial defensive position—what we cannot "fall back" from. More to the point, very few resources in fact are truly irreplaceable: much blood and treasure has repeatedly been wasted in the wake of catastrophic crises because of failures to identify "hidden" resiliency and redundancies ahead of time.

Giving actors the tools to create their own ad hoc fall-back position has the considerable advantage of attenuating "stun effects" commonly provoked by catastrophic crises. It enables them better to absorb the shock caused by the loss of the normal resources that underpin our systems. Plans that are premised on the inevitability of bad news make it easier for leaders and public alike to anticipate it and react to it.

Of course, simply enabling the restoration of individual rationality and the identification of latent resources is not enough to recreate a workable system in the wake of a catastrophic crisis. The juxtaposition of individuals trying to save themselves, or tapping haphazardly into alternate resources, does not amount to a coherent crisis response. A resource-based response can only be **systemically coherent** if each actor is aware of the "building blocks" *provided by others*, and knows which "alternate resources" will be crucial to them.

International crises illustrate this point most clearly. In her book *Role Reversal: Offers of Help From Other Countries in Response to Hurricane Katrina* (Center for Transatlantic Relations, 2006), Anne C. Richard describes a frustrating situation where American authorities did not know what assets foreign countries could provide, and foreign countries were similarly unaware of what was needed on the ground. Therefore, Richard concludes,

> "The international community should develop a uniform list of goods recommended for donation in the event of a crisis… Matrices should be developed to provide information about standards… that are used in various countries… Most useful would be an agreement to stock and use a shortlist of the same emergency supplies, so that there is never any question about the utility of what is being offered."

Similarly, at the domestic level, planning should focus on identifying very clearly the alternate resources that each actor can bring to bear on the response effort, and on laying the ground rules for an efficient sharing of them. Again, when Katrina overwhelmed "behavior-based" plans, actors were forced to define new behaviors unconstrained by pre-agreed standards (i.e. virtually anarchical), and without a clear understanding of available alternate resources, or their respective importance to other actors. Thus, the public sector often resorted to "commandeering" private sector resources such as fuel or water, in order to address global priorities that it felt trumped the local efforts of private companies—to the extent that some among them ended up procuring more emergency resources than they needed, merely to prevent their own efforts from being compromised by outside "predatory" behaviors.

System-wide awareness of alternate resources and of their degree of importance to other actors is not limited to the operational level, i.e. to physical resources such as fuel, power or communication systems. On a strategic plane, the same remarks apply as well: but this time what is meant by "resources" is for instance the **capacity to lead, or civic responsibility**. In the same way that (as Anne Richard highlights) international and domestic actors should know ahead of time what resources are needed and available from others, and how to transfer and combine them, international and domestic plans should start with a strategic outlook based on "building blocks" of another kind: namely the "areas of systemic/civic responsibility" that each major actor acknowledges as its own.

The limits of behavior-based planning are evident at this level as well. Following catastrophic crises, governments will often call for others, especially the private sector, to take on larger swaths of responsibility: in other words, government plans will prescribe a certain course of action to the private sector, without genuinely taking into account what the latter believes its area of responsibility and action should be (and can be). This artificial construct is bound to collapse as soon as an unconventional crisis hits. We need a planning process that starts from an objective assessment by each major actor, in every sector, of the degree of responsibility within the system that it is equipped to take on as its own, or ready to accept as such. Only then can a proper allocation of tasks be designed among the public, private, and humanitarian sector, before the event strikes. Only then, in its wake, can each actor respond with a clear awareness of the boundaries of its competency and responsibility, and of those of its partners.

Concretely, what is needed is a **global, virtual roundtable of international leaders from all sectors** that will clearly state: "this is what we can do in case of a catastrophic crisis—*any* catastrophic crisis; those are the alternate resources and the hidden resiliencies available to us; this is the area of civic responsibility that we are prepared to take on: no less—but no more." This initial assessment should then be turned into proper building blocks for the constitution of adaptable "post-crisis systems," through the rationalization of exchange and mutual help procedures, along the lines suggested above by Richard, and with the help of academic and other experts who can test whether the resulting system of alternate resources and areas of responsibility can be self-sustaining in case of a major crisis.

Failing to pre-define alternate resources at the operational and strategic levels, i.e. (respectively) physical resources and "areas" of civic responsibility, our modern societies, when unconventional crises overwhelm normal systems and undermine behavior patterns pre-scribed by plans, tend to fall back as a last resort on the military, as the only alternate resource that is visibly available when all else has failed. In the process, military behavior comes to dominate the response environment. Katrina provides a clear example of this turn of events. Systematic recourse to the military, however, is unacceptable. In dem-ocratic polities, it only compounds the dissolution of normal social contracts brought about by the failures of civilian leaders. It is also legally problematic, especially in the U.S. where *Posse Comitatus* prevents or at least limits domestic use of regular forces.

Modern societies cannot confront the risk of catastrophic or hyper-complex crises equipped only with two lines of defense, namely their "normal systems" and a single fall-back position—recourse to military assets. In between those two extremes, civilian leaders from all sectors and across countries must create a denser and more flexible system of defense by coming together to pre-identify alternate resources and areas of civic responsibility, and give victims and responders alike the means to reconstitute ad hoc rational systems in the wake of catastrophic events.

Unconventional Leadership and Response: "Rapid Reflection Forces"

All too often, whether or not they genuinely believe it, public or private-sector leaders build their identity, prestige and power upon the premise that they have clear answers to all potential emergent issues. This attitude is fundamentally part and parcel of a culture that is fostered from the time that future leaders attend elite schools where the onus is put on a veneer of excellence, encyclopedic knowledge, and hard sciences.

Under an armor of plans, command-and-control systems, and actuarial databases that admits no chink, leaders are unsurprisingly reluctant to attend seminars and exercises that will go beyond the testing of preset behaviors, and force them out of their comfort zone.

This culture, indeed, serves complex systems well when they have to address conventional crises. It ensures that minor destabilizations do not compromise the coherence of chains of command, the coordination of stovepiped sectors, or the rationality of decision-making processes. Put on this cultural "autopilot," our systems also have developed very fine techniques for "crisis communication," acknowledging "its crucial importance in today's interconnected world." Other mantras include "situational awareness"—though no one in fact is quite sure what that means—and "public-private partnerships": the important thing, in this respect, being that "you should not be exchanging business cards when a crisis hits."

As we have seen, unconventional events will overwhelm this culture and the lines of defense which it has laid out. When catastrophic or hypercomplex crises hit, a culture that is geared towards preserving the coherence of chains of command and behaviors through inflexible prescriptions is not a strength, but a lethal weakness—as it impedes the creativity, indeed the audacity necessary to respond to chaotic and unpredictable events. Suddenly all frameworks of reference are blurred, including sometimes the identification of the problem. Inconceivable speed and unforeseen domino effects overtake decision-making processes and overwhelm the strongest firewalls. Response efforts must take place among a hypercomplex map of actors whose identity and motivations are unclear. Behavioral plans and retrospective databases instantly become irrelevant, and indeed counterproductive. The leaders' own turf becomes unrecognizable, as it dawns on them that they now find themselves behind enemy lines, that the crisis is calling the shots, and that they need a new map of the environment—which they do not have.

In a word, systemic cultures are challenged at their core—yet culture is the oxygen of systems: so they will systematically hold on to it for dear life, even in the face of its inadequacies. Indeed, it is no exaggeration to claim that systems will rather go down than challenge their culture in order to adapt to the new groundrules set by unconventional events. Fiasco, all too often, is very much an option—indeed, the preferred way out: because fiasco, at least, looks familiar.

Time and again, following such events, official reports take good note of the fact that systemic "frontlines" were overwhelmed like so many Maginot lines. Yet, these reports rarely extract themselves from the very same cultural paradigms: indeed most are content to lay the blame at the door of "lack of resources," "lack of communication," "lack of coordination," and simply ask for more assets and more training in the future. In any event, among smoldering ruins of failed systems, one thing is certain, and provides the ultimate consolation and smoke-screen: firefighters and armed forces will have behaved "heroically" throughout the crisis.

This does not challenge nearly enough prevailing leadership cultures and mechanisms.

Based on this premise, Electricité de France—the largest utility in Europe, and main producer of nuclear power worldwide—has decided to act. Simply put, its efforts have aimed to foster a new culture and re-organize crisis management cells to the effect that the group's leaders, when planning for or responding to an unconventional event, do not rush towards answers first, but put themselves in a position to figure out *what the good questions are.*

Alongside "normal" crisis management cells, which operate under considerable time pressure, and confront the granularity of emerging events, EDF has put in place an adjacent team, the "Rapid Reflection Force." The RRF adopts a different timeframe, and focuses on the big picture. Its purpose is to be a "window" that will enable crisis managers to see and hear information that otherwise would not have featured on their radar screen.

It also aims to feed crucial questions, and the lineaments of answers, into the normal crisis cell, at critical junctures:

- **What is the essence of the problem?** Paradoxically, when unconventional events strike, normal crisis response cells have to react without a clear (or judicious) understanding of the type of event they are confronting, at least initially—and sometimes throughout the crisis. Left to their own devices, leaders tend to misdiagnose the crisis, and stick to this initial conclusion against all evidence to the contrary, as giving a label—any label—to an unconventional event at least grants them the comfort of pulling out the corresponding plan from the shelves. The RRF, on the other hand, is in a position to sift through the confusing mass of data at hand to determine more exactly what the crisis truly is about—and do so through all phases of its development, as unconventional events can mutate as time goes by.

- **What crucial pitfalls** must be avoided at all costs, especially in the early days of response efforts? Experience has proved that leaders confronted with hypercomplex crises tend to behave like the captain of a ship in a storm that desperately sets the course toward a misleading beacon lit by coastal "wreckers": they rush to the traps of old and trusted answers that in the new environment are actually counter-productive, and only realize their mistake when it is too late.

- **Who are the stakeholders?** Again, in an unconventional event, "normal" crisis cells will use old maps of actors that do not in fact apply. Stakeholders will not be those that leaders expect, or are used to interacting with.

- **What initiatives** or creative suggestions could enable leaders to change the dynamics of the chaotic environment to their advantage? Such initiatives can best be devised by the RRF, as they require a "big-picture" perspective that conventional crisis cells cannot adopt, and tend to fly in the face of common wisdom.

EDF's RRF typically includes four to six people, including charismatic leaders. The make-up of the team has been described as a combination of "artists" and "doers." Its composition and balance varies depending on the crisis at hand: several formats of the RRF are available and have been tested.

"Artists" can be sociologists, communication specialists, or former managers—their actual background matters less than their capacity to think out-of-the-box, and the fact that they are not subject to "stun effects" when an unconventional event occurs. They are creative, audacious, unconstrained by "common wisdom," and intellectually comfortable with the "unthinkable." They can think across boundaries, irrespective of the firewalls and stovepipes that exist in the normal operating processes of a company.

Meanwhile, the "doers" have an equally important role. Their job is to translate the ideas of the "artists" into robust, workable proposals. Indeed, the most crucial—and most challenging—part of the RRF setup is the link between the Reflection Force and the "normal" crisis team. Timing is of the essence: it would be counterproductive for the RRF to flood the crisis manager with premature or ill-timed insights, when he or she is confronting the granularity of emergent events under considerable time pressure. It is incumbent upon the RRF to identify the appropriate and crucial moments when it should turn to him or her and lay out its analysis with respect to long-term perspective and unforeseen challenges.

This is far from easy—especially in traditionally "vertical" organizations that foster the cultural paradigm that "leaders are supposed to act, not to raise doubts." Indeed, when EDF first implemented the RRF concept at the beginning of 2006, nothing guaranteed that it could succeed. However, it has since tested its mettle, and shown its value, in the course of several crisis exercises and actual events.

Incremental changes in leadership culture have been one of the RRF's most valuable outcomes. As the confidence level grew between it and the normal crisis cell, managers from the latter became increasingly comfortable *asking* the RRF to answer emerging or "unthinkable" questions. The relationship between the RRF and the crisis cell has become a two-way street.

Based on this successful experience, EDF today is eager to connect with European and U.S. companies in order to share, discuss, and improve its model. Our participants' positive response to EDF's efforts convinced us that the second phase of our project should focus on further exploring and broadening the RRF concept.

Reforming the Culture of Leadership: a Generational Challenge

Of course, all proposals for reform and action will fall on deaf ears if leaders simply fail to prioritize the issue of emergency management—which, as many participants noted with dismay, they do all too often. A prerequisite to any other drive for reform must be to educate and lobby leaders from all sectors in order to help them acknowledge, and familiarize themselves with, the threats posed by unconventional events. However, as a participant put it, "there are not a lot of votes in emergency management": therefore, this effort toward a cultural and educational shift is most wisely directed at *future* leaders.

As noted above, the current "managerial" culture of leadership, with its emphasis on top-down command-and-control, rules and regulations, bureaucratic stovepipes, and behavioral plans, is so prevalent in part because it is most often fostered by the elite schools that not only train leaders, but also provide them with a fundamental sense of individual and social identity.

Many of our participants, when teaching "crisis management" classes, have noted with some dismay that the educational system in which they had to operate (including the expectation of students themselves) was not conducive, indeed was hostile to unconventional questions, or to the analysis of past catastrophic events that overwhelmed the best laid-out lines of defense.

Setting up our platform and organizing a seminar at Johns Hopkins University's School of Advanced International Studies enabled us to emphasize this educational dimension of the needed reform of leadership.

Of course, educational systems are characterized by considerable inertia. In the field of unconventional events, we cannot expect that a highly visible "epistemological revolution," i.e. a new "$E = MC^2$" moment, will force radical changes in curricula, and thereby educational practice. Change can only be incremental. On the other hand, precisely because elite schools in Western systems are so few in numbers, and foster coherent intellectual outlooks among current students and alumni in ubiquitous positions of power, even slight modifications in their educational program and practice could go a long way toward reforming the culture of leadership.

In addition, elite educational institutions now exist in a globalized world, and are subject to intense competition. Therefore, the most promising way to break their conservative inertia is for a highly visible and respected school to reform its curriculum, to include unconventional analyses of catastrophic and hypercomplex events.

Conclusion: Phase II

In 2006-2007, the first phase of our project aimed to build a network, propose a common diagnosis, and create mutually intelligible semantics. Methodologically, the priority went to "forcing participants out of their comfort zone," and to finding common ground among participants from various sectors and countries, rather than dwell on differences among their respective experiences.

The success of this initial phase enabled us to develop the "toolbox" that we had set out to create. In 2007-2008, we then moved on to tackle the concrete and specific unconventional issues that confronted our partners, in order to lay out practical solutions.

This policy-oriented approach had several important consequences.

First, we launched an effort to collect recommendations from our partners with respect to their concrete priorities in the field of unconventional or hypercomplex crises, so that the Center for Transatlantic Relations could take their suggestions on board as it developed the project. Priority in this consultation process was given to our financial sponsors, but we also heard from all other participants.

Second, our network was extended to include more leaders that could act upon our policy recommendations: most notably, current policy-makers, from both sides of the Atlantic. Our partners' generous support gave us enough financial visibility to ensure that our network could indeed be strengthened as planned. Again, the momentum that our project acquired in 2007 enabled us to reach out to Europeans and Americans in roughly similar numbers, and make sure that both sides equally contributed to our work and acted upon its conclusions.

As in 2006-2007, our work in the following year hinged upon a seminar that we planned to hold in March 2008, in Washington, D.C. However, the evolution in the spirit and purpose of our project meant that it would not replicate the format of the initial event. The priority now was not to set up a broad dialogue and challenge common wisdom—as this had already been achieved. We could therefore turn to formats that would be more conducive to the elaboration of practical answers and proposals for action, e.g. by combining plenary sessions with topical roundtables where sub-groups of cross-sector and international specialists would convene to examine specific issues; as well as scenario-based exercises that would not only show the limits of conventional response mechanisms, but elicit innovative processes aiming to reform them.

As noted above, our project from the start has strived to remain as unconventional or unorthodox as the crises it aims to examine and confront. This report would be counter-productive if it ran counter to this philosophy. The pages that precede do not purport to lay out a "final word," just as the project they describe did not claim to produce it.

"This is not the end. It is not even the beginning of the end. But it is, perhaps, the end of the beginning."

Annex I

Partners and Participants

In 2007, our event's format imposed a limit on the number of participants, which we initially set at about thirty. We were careful that they be drawn from the public and private sectors, NGOs, media opinion-shapers, academia, and private citizens groups—based on the guiding principles that cross-sector dialogue and multi-disciplinarity were essential to our approach, and that participants should be selected on the basis of their experience, insights, and open-mindedness, rather than their affiliation or their expertise on traditional crisis-management procedures. We also aimed to ensure a balance among European and North-American participants.

Private Sector

Pierre Béroux
> Senior Vice President, Risk Control Directorate, Electricité de France.

Kathryn Brown
> Senior Vice President, Public Policy Development and International Government Relations, Verizon.

Cristin Flynn Goodwin
> Policy Counsel, specialist of Emergency Preparedness, Microsoft Corporation. Former Director of Homeland Security, BellSouth.

Michael Hickey
> Vice President, Government Affairs & National Security Policy, Verizon.

John Hoeft
> Vice President and General Counsel, Veolia Transportation.

Deane Johanis
> Manager, Emergency Planning, Greater Toronto Airports Authority.

Janice Maragakis
> Vice President, Corporate Communications, Accor North America.

Robert Noonan
> Managing Director, Crisis Management and Business Continuity, Corporate & Investment Banking Division, Société Générale.

Public Sector

Thomas Day
> Senior Vice-President, Government Relations, United States Postal Service.

John Farmer
> Former Senior Counsel and Team Leader for the 9/11 Commission. Former Attorney General for the State of New Jersey.

Uwe Christian Fischer
> Plans, Programs and Policy Department, German Ministry of the Interior.

Michael Theilmann
> Senior Liaison Director from the Canadian Government (Public Safety and Emergency Preparedness) to the U.S. Department of Homeland Security. Former Chief of Operational Readiness, Counter-Terrorism Division, Department of the Solicitor General of Canada.

James Young
> Special Advisor to the Minister, Public Safety and Emergency Preparedness, Government of Canada.

Non-Governmental & Humanitarian Organizations

Nan Buzard
> Senior Director, International Disaster Response, American Red Cross.

David Carden
> Heard, Early Warning & Contingency Planning Unit, OCHA (United Nations Office for the Coordination of Humanitarian Affairs).

Don Eberly
> Former Senior Counselor for International Civil Society at USAID and Director of Private Sector Outreach and Coordination for tsunami reconstruction at the U.S. State Department. Former Director of Social Policy and Private Assistance for Iraq at the Pentagon and U.S. State Department.

George Haddow
> Acting Director, Domestic Emergency Management Program, Save The Children. Adjunct Professor, Institute for Crisis, Disaster and Risk Management, George Washington University. Former Deputy Chief of Staff to former FEMA Director James Lee Witt.

Joel Starr
> Chief of Staff and Legislative Director, Legislative and Public Affairs, USAID.

Simon Strickland
> Senior Policy Advisor, United Nations System Influenza Coordination (UNSIC).

Academia, Think-Tanks and Consulting Groups

Sandra Bell
> Director, Homeland Security and Resilience Department, Royal United Services Institute for Defence and Security Studies, UK.

Mike Granatt
> Partner, Luther Pendragon. Former Director of the UK's Cabinet Office Civil Crisis Management Unit (Civil Contingencies Secretariat).

David Heyman
> Director and Senior Fellow, Homeland Security Program, Center for Strategic and International Studies (CSIS).

Arnold Howitt
> Executive Director, Taubman Center for State and Local Government, and Co-Chair, Executive Program on Crisis Management, Kennedy School of Government, Harvard University.

Patrick Lagadec
> Director of Research, Ecole Polytechnique, France.

Robert Liscouski
> President and CEO, ContentAnalyst. Former Assistant Secretary for Infrastructure Protection, U.S. Department of Homeland Security. Senior Fellow, Homeland Security Policy Institute, George Washington University.

Leo Michel
> Senior Research Fellow, National Defense University.

Didier Ranchon
> Vice-President, European Business Development, GEOS International. Former Head of the French Foreign Ministry's Emergency Response and Tracking Center.

Samuel Wells
> Associate Director, and Director of West European Studies, Woodrow Wilson International Center for Scholars.

Robert Whalley
> Consulting Senior Fellow, International Institute for Strategic Studies (IISS), UK. Former Director for Counter Terrorism and Intelligence, Home Office, UK Government. Former Head of Emergency Planning Division, Home Office.

Annex II
Seminar Program, March 14-16, 2007

The first phase of our project, in 2006-2007, aimed to turn a collection of networks and individuals into a coherent platform for reflection and action; lay out our analysis of the challenges posed by catastrophic crises with transatlantic implications, and use it to create enough common ground—though not necessarily a consensus—among our partners' different viewpoints to enable a balanced dialogue; and develop the first lineaments of concrete proposals for action, which we proposed to develop in further stages of the project.

This hinged initially on a two-day seminar that we organized at Johns Hopkins University's School of Advanced International Studies in Washington, D.C., on March 14-16, 2007.

Specifically, the focus of this event was to:

- share cutting-edge analyses of the main challenges posed by unconventional crises

- highlight common vulnerabilities and interdependencies on a transatlantic scale, by emphasizing the extent to which the destabilization of certain critical infrastructures in Europe would instantly affect the United States, and vice-versa

- exchange "lessons observed," intuitions and questions drawn from the participants' experience of recent unconventional crises

- put forward innovative approaches in strategic, operational, and cultural terms that may enable to better prepare for, respond to and recover from such events: especially with respect to the relationship among the private and public sectors and NGOs, as well as among transnational, national, and local Homeland Security institutions

- open avenues for further enquiry, analysis and training, and initiate a network among participants in order to explore them.

Consistent with our wish to promote unconventional, innovative analysis, the seminar did not follow a "panel-and-audience" format; rather, we proposed a more inclusive approach whereby all experts invited were encouraged to share (off-the-record) interrogations, intuitions and proposed roadmaps for progress. We developed a schedule that combined inclusive discussions with an unconventional tabletop simulation exercise in order to highlight issues and challenges in concrete terms. Much time was left to open discussions, as opposed to "magisterial" exposés.

Specifically, the sessions described below did not follow the traditional format whereby time is shared unevenly between a panel and (when time allows) questions and answers. Rather, each topic was framed briefly by "coordinators" who opened the floor for an inclusive discussion on the subject by all participants.

Wednesday, March 14, 2007

Welcome Reception

Thursday, March 15, 2007

Welcome Address, Presentation of the Seminar, Sponsors

Dr. Esther Brimmer, Deputy Director of the Center for Transatlantic Relations; **Dr. Erwan Lagadec,** Center for Transatlantic Relations

Dr. Patrick Lagadec, Ecole Polytechnique and IRGC; **Pierre Béroux,** Electricité de France

Kathryn Brown, Senior Vice President, Public Policy Development and International Government Relations, Verizon; **Michael Hickey,** Vice-President Government Affairs & National Security Policy, Verizon

Presentation of Participants

Each participant was asked briefly to introduce themselves, their affiliation, field of expertise, recent crises that they worked on or were involved in, and expectations for the seminar.

Session 1: Unconventional Crises, Unconventional Responses: Towards a Culture of Chaotic Events

Presentation

Exploring paradigm shifts and cultural changes needed to confront chaotic, non-linear, and hypercomplex situations. Presenting the notion of "Rapid Reflection Forces": i.e. teams of experts "parallel" to the incident command center (yet enjoying immediate access to its leaders), tasked with taking a "step back" *vis-à-vis* the urgent requirements of crisis management, and adopting a different timeframe than the first responders, in order to think through strategic posture, anticipate unheeded obstacles, and advise leaders and first responders on these questions at each critical juncture in the response effort. In any given crisis, these experts must especially clarify (1) what the *essence of the problem* is, (2) what the *key traps* to be wary of are, (3) what *unconventional network of actors* needs to be set up, and (4) what *critical initiatives* will put the response effort in the best possible posture early on.

Coordinators:

Patrick Lagadec, Ecole Polytechnique and IRCG

Pierre Béroux, Electricité de France

Discussion

Session 2: New Social Contracts: Inter-Sector Cooperation and the Emergence of New Actors

Presentation

Examining effective allocations of tasks among the public and private sectors, NGOs, the media, and private citizens; and among local, national and transnational organizations (cf. for instance 9/11 in New York City, 2004 Tsunami, Katrina).

Coordinators:

Mike Granatt, Former Director of the UK's Cabinet Office Civil Crisis Management Unit (Civil Contingencies Secretariat)

Cristin Flynn Goodwin, Policy Counsel, Specialist of Emergency Preparedness, Microsoft Corp. Former Director of Homeland Security, BellSouth

John J. Farmer, Former Senior Counsel and New York Team Leader for the 9/11 Commission

Discussion

Session 3: Transnational Vulnerabilities. The Limits and Opportunities of International Cooperation

Presentation

Highlighting common or reciprocal vulnerabilities that bind North America and Europe together (cf. for instance 9/11, SARS outbreak in Toronto, 2006 Transatlantic airliners terrorist plot, avian flu). Exploring the dysfunctional mechanisms of international cooperation in crisis prevention, management and recovery (cf. for instance 2004 Tsunami, Katrina).

Coordinators:

James G. Young, Special Advisor to the Minister, Public Safety and Emergency Preparedness, Government of Canada

Nan Buzard, Director of International Disaster Response, American Red Cross

Didier Ranchon, Vice President, GEOS International. Former Head of the French Foreign Ministry's Emergency Response and Tracking Center

Discussion

Reception at the Canadian Embassy

Hosted by **Kevin O'Shea,** Minister Political Affairs.

Friday, March 16, 2007

Session 4: Unconventional Simulation Exercise

Coordinators: Patrick Lagadec and Mike Granatt

Most "tabletop" simulation exercises follow a common pattern. Organizers prepare a detailed scenario ahead of the event. After its premises are laid out and participants set to work, new information is released on a regular basis, indicating developments brought about in part by the participants' decisions. In their response, participants are expected to conform to a set plan, which the simulation aims to test and rehearse. Finally, a debriefing highlights and examines gaps between the posture and response adopted, and those expected by the organizers and called for by "the plan."

The unconventional type of simulation that we organized, and which we had previously tested with much success, followed an entirely different pattern, as it aimed to train participants to react to the "unthinkable" through out-of-the-box initiatives. The exercise, then, focused on creative questioning, not on the strict observance of given scripts, rules and responses. Experience has shown that this type of preparation is a much more effective way to prevent future "failures of imagination, of initiative, of leadership" than is the traditional approach of testing expanded plans and pre-formatted responses even more comprehensively, when earlier plans and exercises have proven inadequate.

No scenario was prepared in advance. In other words, participants were not asked simply to react to data thrust upon them. First, they were split into groups comprising experts from different backgrounds. Then, with no other constraints than a thematic framework proposed by the organizers, each group was given 45 minutes to prepare a scenario as it saw fit. This could simply consist in the outline of a situation that the group's members found particularly challenging, and/or that is traditionally overlooked by official plans.

The plenary session was reconvened, and organizers briefly presented all suggested scenarios. They then picked the scenario proposed by one group, and tasked a different group with confronting it and developing initial proposals and intuitions, for about 20 minutes.

The lead group was then asked to present its proposed response, examine the difficulties encountered, and highlight lessons or questions arising from them, with all participants— including those who had drawn up the scenario in question. Instead of organizers pointing negatively, and in a "professorial" posture, to hiatuses between responses and a set plan, all participants were therefore invited to comment, in a positive and constructive spirit, on the lead groups' decisions. More emphasis was put on the quality of the *questions* asked by the lead group, than on its ability to apply pre-formatted responses. All participants were also encouraged to pool their questions, intuitions, and proposed roadmaps.

The process was then repeated, with other lead groups successively taking on each of the other scenarios elaborated in the first phase of the simulation.

Session 5: Conclusion: Building a Network, Drawing a Roadmap

Coordinators: Esther Brimmer, Erwan Lagadec, Center for Transatlantic Relations

About the Author

Dr. Erwan Lagadec is a SAIS Foreign Policy Institute Fellow at the Center for Transatlantic Relations. His work focuses on Transatlantic Homeland Security issues and U.S.-EU-NATO military and civil-military relations. A French National, Dr. Lagadec holds a D.Phil. in history from the University of Oxford (2004). He has worked as a research associate for the French Foreign Ministry Policy Planning Staff (2003, 2005). In 2004-5 he was a Public Policy Scholar at the Woodrow Wilson Center and a Visiting Scholar at SAIS, working on French-U.S. relations during the 2003 Iraq Crisis. In 2005-2006 he was a Postdoctoral Fellow and an Affiliate at Harvard University's Center for European Studies, and also worked at the U.S. mission to the EU on NATO-ESDP relations. In the summer of 2007, as a Navy Reserve Officer, he was assigned to the French Permanent Representation to the EU, where he was tasked with developing proposals for the French EU-U.S.-NATO security agenda ahead of the French EU presidency in 2008. He is also a non-resident Visiting Fellow at MIT's Security Studies Program, and a member of the International Institute for Strategic Studies.

In 2005 he co-produced a report on "The Rehabilitation of Civilian Ports in Crisis Situations" for the Délégation aux Affaires Stratégiques at the French Ministry of Defense. He also co-authored a 2006 report for Electricité de France (EDF) and the French Navy Chief of Staff that analyzed the response of Gulf Coast critical infrastructure providers in the wake of Hurricane Katrina.

About the Center

The Paul H. Nitze **School of Advanced International Studies** (SAIS) is one of America's leading graduate schools devoted to the study of international relations. It is based at Johns Hopkins University, one of the nation's premier research universities. SAIS leads the international research activities of the Johns Hopkins-led Center for the Study of High Consequence Event Preparedness and Response (PACER), named as one of the five U.S. National Centers of Excellence in Homeland Security by the U.S. Department of Homeland Security. This group is comprised of seventeen different university institutes across the United States, and studies a range of homeland security challenges. Further information is available at http://www.sais-jhu.edu.

The SAIS **Center for Transatlantic Relations** is a non-profit research center that engages opinion leaders on contemporary challenges facing Europe and North America. The goal of the Center is to strengthen and reorient transatlantic relations to the dynamics of the globalizing world. More information can be found at http://transatlantic.sais-jhu.edu. The Center serves as the coordinator for the American Consortium on European Union Studies (ACES), which is a partnership among five national-capital area universities—American, George Mason, George Washington, Georgetown and Johns Hopkins—to improve understanding of the European Union and U.S.-EU relations. The Consortium has been recognized by the European Commission as the EU Center of Excellence in Washington D.C. CTR also contributed to the creation of the Congressional Caucus on the European Union, and remains closely associated with it.

In 2005 the Center organized and hosted the event *Atlantic Storm*, based on the scenario of a simultaneous biological terrorist attack in Europe and the United States, which included high-profile participants such as Bernard Kouchner and Madeleine Albright. In addition, the Center has published extensively on homeland security issues, e.g. *Transforming Homeland Security: U.S. and European Approaches; Transatlantic Homeland Security? Protecting Society in the Age of Catastrophic Terrorism; Protecting the Homeland: European Approaches to Societal Security —Implications for the United States; Terrorism and International Security; Fighting Terrorism Financing: Transatlantic Cooperation and International Institutions.* and *Role Reversal: Offers of Help from Other Countries in Response to Hurricane Katrina.*